Doing Time with Nehru

Doing Time with Nehru

The Story of an Indian-Chinese Family

YIN MARSH

zubaan

ZUBAAN
an imprint of Kali for Women
128B Shahpur Jat, 1st Floor
NEW DELHI 110 049
Email: contact@zubaanbooks.com
Website: www.zubaanbooks.com

This edition published by Zubaan 2015

10 9 8 7 6 5 4 3 2 1

ISBN 978 93 84757 80 9

Zubaan is an independent feminist publishing house based in New Delhi
with a strong academic and general list. It was set up as an imprint of
India's first feminist publishing house, Kali for Women, and carries
forward Kali's tradition of publishing world quality books to high editorial
and production standards. *Zubaan* means tongue, voice, language, speech
in Hindustani. Zubaan publishes in the areas of the humanities, social
sciences, as well as in fiction, general non-fiction, and books for children
and young adults under its Young Zubaan imprint.

Typeset in Adobe Caslon Pro 11/14.4 by Jojy Phillip, New Delhi 110 015
Printed at Raj Press, R-3 Inderpuri, New Delhi 110 012

I dedicate this memoir to my father who showed me how to laugh during trying times, and to my mother for her amazing capability and efforts to get our release.

I further dedicate this memoir to fellow internees whose lives changed in an instant, and the difficult times they endured in silence for the past fifty years.

Contents

Introduction

PAYAL BANERJEE

I find it most appropriate to begin this Introduction with an excerpt from the book:

> …three Indian police officers showed up. They were in khaki uniforms and appeared unemotional. They told us they had come to take us away and that we should be prepared to be away for a long time. They didn't take kindly to our questions and answered brusquely. They didn't know where we were being taken or how long we would be gone. We needed to take warm clothes, bedding, a few pots and pans, and other essentials needed to exist for many months…. I looked at our neighbours who were watching us being carted off like common criminals: a grandmother…her thirteen-year-old granddaughter and her eight-year-old grandson. They didn't look at us as old friends and neighbours. It was a different look, one of astonishment. It also seemed to say we were outsiders. A flood of simultaneous emotions overwhelmed me: bewilderment, fear of the unknown, and a feeling of shame: shame for being Chinese.

Yin Marsh's powerful memoir *Doing Time with Nehru* orients our attention to the lives of people of Chinese origin in India. Living in the country as citizens, long term residents, neighbours, or as the kin of Indians, bound to them by blood or marital vows—the Chinese Indians confronted the ordeals of mass arrests, incarceration and internment, and the repercussions of being newly classified, by law, as 'enemy aliens' following the onset of the India-China war in 1962. *Doing Time with Nehru* allows us therefore to absorb and contemplate the political, social, and deeply personal significance of the events that intersected violently with the lives of the Chinese, events that have for over 60 years remained unacknowledged in the nation's imaginary of its own history, politics, and sense of self.

It is critical to point out that the people of Chinese ancestry in question here were an integral part of India's very own diverse and multi-ethnic population. Emerging from a long and rich history of migration spanning well over a century since the early 1800s, people of Chinese descent in the country at the time of the 1962 war came to represent a remarkable social diversity that went beyond the indices of occupation or class. A large number had migrated in their own lifetime, while others were born in India and had grown up as second or third generation Chinese-Indians; newcomers were sometimes married to old-timers; many maintained social ties with relatives in China, whereas others were too far removed in time to do so but nonetheless preserved Chinese cultural practices. Especially in places like Assam, mixed family heritage was not uncommon because of inter-marriage with Indians over the decades, which in turn produced multi-ethnic extended families related by ties of kinship. Members of the Chinese community were fluent in Assamese, Bengali, Khasi, Nepali, Hindi, and English, which reflected their cultural links to the various ethno-linguistic spaces of India. Some had long completed the formality of obtaining Indian citizenship after independence, whereas others had not, which is hardly surprising given the temporal proximity of the early 1960s to the time when India finally became decolonized and formally acquired the designation of an independent republic.

Following the 1962 war, the Indian state, and the public, however, disavowed unequivocally this long and enmeshed socio-cultural belonging of the Chinese community in the country, thus violating the integrity of their roots and history in India. An ensemble of newly-passed laws, such as the Foreigner's Law (Application and Amendment) Ordinance (October 30, 1962), the Foreigner's (Internment) Order (November 3, 1962), the Foreigners Law Act (passed on November 26, 1962), and the Foreigner's Order (issued on January 14, 1963) authorized arrests, repatriation, deportation, and other violations of civil rights of those identified as having any Chinese ancestry. Each law targeted different aspects of life, legal status, and disentitlements. Modelled after U.S. President Franklin D. Roosevelt's Executive Order No. 9066, which authorized the detention of Japanese Americans in camps during World War II, the Indian government's Foreigner's (Internment) Order (November 3, 1962) in particular authorized the detention and incarceration of the Chinese at the Central Internment camp in Deoli, Rajasthan, and a prison in Nowgong (today Nagaon), Assam.[1] The Foreigner's Law Act (November 26, 1962) and the Foreigner's Order (issued on January 14,

1963), on the other hand, erased distinctions between people in China, a country with which India was at war, and the Chinese living in India, who represented the demography and cultural ethos of the nation-state's existing multi-ethnic population. New amendments in the legal definition of foreigners were introduced to classify persons adjudged to bear any measure of Chinese ancestry as 'aliens,' and in this case, 'aliens' from an enemy nation. Those who had Indian citizenship found their status rescinded. Cohen and Leng's analysis of the implications conveyed by these laws, as they reconfigured completely what it meant to be a person of Chinese ancestry in India, is highly instructive and worth our attention:

> President Radhakrishnan promulgated on October 30, 1962, the Foreigner's Law (Application and Amendment) Ordinance, which made the Registration of Foreigner's Act of 1939 and the Foreigner's Act of 1946, and all rules and orders issued thereunder, applicable to 'any person not of Indian origin who was at birth a citizen or subject of any country at war with, or committing external aggression against India'. Another order issued on the same day suspended for the duration of the emergency the right of such persons, as well as foreigners, to move any court for the enforcement of basic constitutional protections against the arbitrary deprivation of life and liberty. In order to effectuate the Indian government's intention to subject all Indian citizens of Chinese origin to both the October 30 measures, their definition of 'person' was soon broadened to make the regulatory scheme applicable to 'any person who, or either whose parents, or any of whose grandparents was at any time a citizen or subject of any country at war with, or committing external aggression against, India'. This became

the definition of 'person of Chinese origin' as that term was used in subsequent measures, such as the Foreigner's (Restricted Areas) Order, 1963, mentioned above. The effect of these measures was to deny the almost 900 Indian citizens of Chinese origin the benefits of citizenship and to subject them to the same restrictions and controls as Chinese aliens.[2]

Under the provisions of "The Control of Internees' Property Order," issued by the Ministry of Commerce and Industry, a state appointed custodian seized the assets and business accounts of those interned in camps. Furthermore, a corresponding climate of anti-Chinese intolerance, suspicion, and violence saturated the public realm, which, by most accounts, was nearly unprecedented before the war.[3]

Marsh's narrative documents the lived, tangible experiences of her family as they were forced to inhabit and conform to the country's new legal construction of a Chinese person and its dire consequences: being arrested in thousands and sent to local prisons or makeshift jails without charge or trial, before being sent to the Central Internment Camp at the other end of the country. Although these arrests were conducted most comprehensively in the Northeastern regions near the border (Assam's Makum and Digboi, Shillong in Meghalaya, West Bengal's Darjeeling, Kurseong, and Kalimpong areas), thousands were taken into custody from large cities like Calcutta, Bombay, Delhi, Kanpur, Jamshedpur, and other parts as well. Small children, teenagers, the elderly, pregnant women, and in many cases Indian spouses and children, were detained without any charges. Those served with 'Quit India' orders had to leave the country on a month's notice, and failure to comply resulted in imprisonment. According to official data, the Government of India repatriated about 1,665 Chinese internees along with their 730 dependents to China by September of 1963. Forcible deportations continued till December of 1967. About 7,500 people, not forcibly deported or repatriated, left India between 1962 and 1967 (for China, Hong Kong, Pakistan, Taiwan, Japan, Australia, U.K., U.S., and Canada). The actual number of people impacted in every category—arrested, imprisoned, repatriated, and interned—was of course inestimably higher than figures quoted in official documents. This was the violence of the state: an institution that carried the legitimacy and legislative authority of the nation, and could thus mobilize resources at its disposal to implement the technologies of repression in the name of the people, and the sanctity and security of their being and territory.

At public talks and presentations based on my research on the Chinese internment, I have been asked the following question: how might one explain the relatively small number—2165—of Chinese Indians who were interned in Deoli, given that clearly the population was much larger than that? This question demands a bit of contemplation. If we were to focus primarily on arriving at a reasonable explanation for the apparent smallness of the number of detainees at 2000 plus, given the size of India's Chinese community, a plausible approach would be to consider the seemingly diminutive character of the figure as an outcome of at least two intersecting forces, for which there is some evidence: (one) the arbitrary nature of state action as well as limitations placed on the implementation of the laws given the obvious constraints of available resources, such as adequate manpower or infrastructure to execute mass arrests, house those detained, organize transportation, coordinate timely communication, etc. and, (two) the ability of some Chinese, especially those in urban areas, to negotiate to some measure a deferral or postponement of arrests, or access to release documents, though the use of social contacts and class privilege. But then, there is ample evidence, in *Doing Time with Nehru* and elsewhere, that class privilege could not always ensure these advantages and often exposed the prosperous to even greater exploitation. Ethnographic material from Assam has shown, for example, that police officers displayed an express preference for arresting those with property and businesses with the ulterior motive of acquiring personal control over such assets or breaking into areas of commerce in which the Chinese had long-established expertise, such as carpentry and the tea industry. A better place to start questioning the detention is a political one. The number of detainees at 2000+ in Deoli signals not whether or not the number is a small number or a big one, but instead, points to the near absolute and arbitrary power of the state to arrest and detain based on what it deems appropriate and feasible. It is this power that contributed to Deoli's final head-count, which could just as easily have been 1,000, or even 10,000, given the size of the Chinese-Indian community and the scale of the arrests. The characteristics of the people ultimately sent to the camp from among those apprehended does not signal any precise organizing principle, rationale, or precondition, or anything that can fully explain their internment on the basis of markers that could distinguish those interned from those who were held in custody in jails elsewhere, or kept under surveillance. Those interned, as is revealed in this memoir and in other sources, represented a cross-section of the community. Among those included, it is important to mention, were an overwhelming number of people who constituted a demography that one might deem to be non-threatening: infants, children, and the elderly. A few of the internees were the non-Chinese kin of mixed-families. Counterparts to the camp's entire population could be found elsewhere in places like West Bengal, being subjected to other forms of state repression or public harassment, but free nonetheless, while thousands of others were in local jails.[4] Clearly, they could also very well have been conscripted for internment. The final count of detainees in Deoli thus does not represent a calibrated or systematic figure, and its logic is contained nowhere in its calibration. The number cannot *explain* each individual's detention, nor the *total number* detained. Marsh's memoir helps us understand that it is not the final tally of detainees, but rather the fact of detention itself, that reveals the centrality of the state's dispensations of its legitimate authority and the scope for cruelty therein. To a large extent then, for the state, the exact number of those detained was somewhat ancillary to another consideration: namely, the grave symbolic value asserted in the demarcation of difference by incarceration. For those interned, the magnitude of being consigned to Deoli spilled over tens of thousands of interconnected lives as families were forcibly separated and displaced, with inestimable consequences. Pramila Das, who also answers to her Chinese name Leong Lin Chi, is one among hundreds of Assamese Chinese engaged, as we speak now, in the protracted search for deported relatives.[5] Just six years of age when her parents were transported to China from Deoli, she has spent a lifetime seeking to be reunited.

As the experiences of Chinese-Indians show, this aggressive and immediate nature of state violence unleashed during the war transmuted over time into an equally potent form of what Gyanendra Pandey calls "routine violence." It might be useful to provide the following description from Pandey's work to place into perspective how those who remained in India encountered a more prolonged and quotidian form of violence that filtered just as insidiously into the day-to-day organization of life.

> ...we must recognize violence not only in its most spectacular, explosive, visible moments, but also in its most disguised forms—in our day-to-day behavior, the way we construct and respond to neighbors as well as strangers, in the books and magazines we read, the films we see, and the conversations and silences in which we participate....the routine violence involved in the construction of naturalized nations, of natural communities and histories, majorities and minorities.[6]

The exigencies of wartime persecutions did not end with the war; they lingered and lived on well over the next three decades and beyond, as the laws were not repealed. Seized property, assets, and personal belongings were never returned, stolen or mislaid by neighbours entrusted with their supervision or by state officials serving as custodians. For those who could return to their former homes, the financial devastation inflicted upon them got magnified by the denial of citizenship, which was not restored until the late 1990s. Ordinances that mandated the Chinese to report to Indian authorities at close intervals, stayed valid. Further, the new requirement of renewing annual permits to live in India ensured the certainty of harassment and extortion at the hands of state agents responsible for processing relevant paperwork. The imposition of surveillance and restrictions on free movement without permits for more than 24 hours, even within a few miles of one's own home or registered address, remained in effect until the early 1980s; the specific order against free movement was removed in 1996.[7] The last group of internees at Deoli was released in 1967. Indian films and media secured an ideological and cultural consensus against the Chinese by representing China, and all Chinese, as deceitful, predatory, and ruthless.[8] For many Chinese who stayed back in India, the longevity of these policies changed forever their relationship to the places they called home. The war and its aftermath left deep psychic and visceral imprints, often of fear and trauma, which carried over for the generation interned and deported, despite the passage of time into the 21st century and lives lived in places like the U.S., Canada, or elsewhere.

Scholars working in the field of South Asia, in particular historians, anthropologists, and sociologists working on India, have produced a formidable body of work devoted to the study of the many manifestations of violence in the country's post-colonial period: the massacres during the Partition, systemic violence against religious minorities, the rise of Hindutva, discriminatory intersections of caste, class, and gender/sexual hierarchies, in particular Adivasi and Dalit marginalization, and of course, the structural violence of poverty. Far from representing a narrow engagement with individual communities or regional case studies concerning the tenors of violence, this scholarship offers deep reflections about the many articulations of modern political and institutionalized violence, its discourses and practices inflecting the realms of nationalism, identity, economic policy, or state bureaucracy. And yet, the violation upon violations that the Chinese in India encountered during the 1962 war and later over a course of 60 years have not received the scholarly appraisal that this critical chapter in Indian history deserves.[9] The profoundness of this void is made even more striking when one juxtaposes the tremendous weight that the India-China war has carried in shaping the scope of India's nationalism, military and security policies, and geo-political strategies. To be sure, the war itself has received considerable attention, judging by the number of publications, many academic, on the political history of the war, the border, coverage of military events preceding the war, diplomatic exchanges, as well as the substantial number of memoirs written by Indian military officers and diplomats, indicating an enduring interest on the topic. However, none are attentive to what *Doing Time with Nehru* makes visible.[10] There is violence in being excluded from recognition, and in the case of India's Chinese, this violence is woefully reenacted in being unacknowledged in the registers of the social sciences, and in the historical and political writings on modern India.

Yin Marsh not only breaks the silence from within the community, but also, and even more importantly, establishes a repository that can be accessed to produce a more comprehensive view of Indian history.[11] As I have noted elsewhere, her memoir "leaves evidence of the visceral and emotional, the simultaneity of the deeply private and immensely public encounters of everyday harassment on the streets, termination of employment, police raids at home, destruction of property, unexplained arrests, and numerous other forms of anti-Chinese state repression, which show

how the Chinese in India occupied the vortex of what constituted India's political explorations of its sovereignty as a post-colonial nation."[12] Seen from this perspective, Marsh's work is to be read as a bequeathal, one that can begin to fill the epistemic voids and political silences concerning a community that was within and integral to India's social and cultural composition. Emplaced in *Doing Time with Nehru* is the history of the Chinese in India—an integral part of the nation's history—and also, dare I say, an inauguration of the hope that Indians share, with respect and humility, the task that lies ahead of researching further and reckoning with this history, and not leave it entirely to the Chinese-Indians.

Gangtok, Sikkim (a few miles from Darjeeling, Yin Marsh's hometown in India). August 2015

Notes

1. References to the Central Internment Camp in Deoli and a second internment facility at Nowgong are to be found in communications between the governments of India and China. See: Government of India. 1964. *Notes, memoranda and letters exchanged between the governments of India and China: White Paper, July 1963–1964*, no. 10, pp. 65–66. Delhi: GOI Press.

2. Cohen, Alan Jerome and Shao-chuan Leng. 1972. 'The Sino-Indian Dispute over the Internment and Detention of Chinese Nationals', in A.J. Cohen (ed.), *China's Practice of International Law: Some Case Studies*, pp. 75. Cambridge: Harvard University Press.

3. Although the anti-Chinese laws were passed in the war's

wake no doubt, it is important to point out however that archival evidence indicates that as early as in 1960 the Indian government had at least considered, and in some instances implemented at a very preliminary level, certain measures to observe and monitor members of the Chinese community in India, especially in North Bengal. See: Amit Das Gupta's chapter in Lüthi, Lorenz M. and Amit Das Gupta. eds. *Sino-Indian Border War, 1962*. (Volume under consideration at Cambridge University Press).

4. See: Banerjee, Payal. 'The Chinese in India: Internment, Nationalism, and the Embodied Imprints of State Action', in L.M. Lüthi and A.D. Gupta (eds.), *Sino-Indian Border War, 1962*. (Volume under consideration at Cambridge University Press).

5. See: PTI. 2015. 'Assamese of Chinese Origin Facing Severe Identity Crisis', *The Economic Times*, 17 May. http://articles.economictimes.indiatimes.com/2015-05-17/news/62276819_1_tinsukia-tea-industry-assamese (accessed 19 May 2015). Regarding the title of this article, it is important to state that: by evoking the notion of 'identity crisis,' the title pathologizes the Chinese in India, rather than question the policies from which emerged the crisis of prolonged, inhuman separation from loved ones. It is also important to note here that many people of Chinese ancestry were forced to adopt "Indian" sounding names as means of securing some protection against persecution.

6. Pandey, Gyanendra. 2006. *Routine Violence: Nations, Fragments, Histories*, pp. 8. Stanford: Stanford University Press.

7. Dutta, Ananya. 2012. 'A Psyche Shaped by Conflict', *The Hindu*, 18 November. http://www.thehindu.com/news/national/other-states/apsyche-shaped-by-conflict/article4106426.ece. (accessed 13 June 2014).

8. See: Banerjee, P. 2007. 'Chinese Bodies in Fire: Interpreting the Refractions of Ethnicity, Gender, Sexuality, and Citizenship in Post-colonial India's Memories of the Sino-Indian War', *China Report*, 43 (4): 437–563; and, Uberoi, P. 2011. 'China in Bollywood', *Contributions to Indian Sociology*, 45: 315–342.

9. For an overview of the existing scholarly work on the topic, I would refer the reader to the following:

   - *Ibid.*, p. xxii.

   - Banerjee, *op. cit.*, p. xxi.

   - Li, Kwai-Yun. 2011. 'Deoli Camp: An Oral History of Chinese Indians from 1962 to 1966'. Unpublished Master's thesis, Ontario Institute for Studies in Education, University of Toronto.

   - Bonnerjee, Jayani. 2010. 'Neighborhood, City, Diaspora: Identity and Belonging for Calcutta's Anglo-Indian and Chinese Communities'. Unpublished Ph.D. thesis, University of London.

   - Oxfeld, Ellen. 1993. *Blood, Sweat, and Mahjong: Family and Enterprise in an Overseas Chinese Community*. Ithaca: Cornell University Press.

   - *The Legend of Fat Mama*. 2005, motion picture. Rafeeq Ellias. Kolkata.

   - Chowdhury, Rita. 2010. *Makam*. Guwahati: Jyoti Prakashan.

   - Chatterjee, G. 1996. 'Goodbye Chinatown', *Far Eastern Economic Review*, 159(20): 28–29.

   - Sengupta, S. 1993. 'Marginality and Segregation: A Concept of Socio-political Environment in Urban Setting', *Man in India*, 73(1): 41–47."

10. See: Banerjee, *op. cit*, p. xxii.

11. I would also stress the urgent need for this scholarship, in light of certain recent developments in India. For example, there have been attempts by the Hindu Right to revive a national focus on the India-China war but by re-fashioning school textbooks such that the message emphasized from a review of the India-China war's outcome can be the valiance of the Indian soldiers and the sacrifice of the fallen heroes, as opposed to one that dwells upon India's defeat.

12. See: Banerjee, *op. cit.*, p. xxi.

Author's Note

Since my memoir is about events that took place more than four decades ago, I am using the old Wade-Giles spelling for Chinese names of people and cities, which may be more familiar to readers. I also use the old-Indian spelling: for instance, Calcutta instead of Kolkata.

Foreword

I have watched my mother grow into the most amazing storyteller. When she speaks, people lean in, the room becomes quieter, and the anticipation is palpable. She wasn't always this way. She used to avoid speaking of her history—or about herself altogether—giving only enough details to keep her inquirers satisfied or confused enough to stop probing. Perhaps her privacy made me all the more curious.

As a child I used to get glimpses into her past: mention of a cruel nun at the Darjeeling boarding school, where she lived from age four to twelve, her grandmother somewhat constricted by her bound feet, her father taken suddenly and inexplicably to jail, and the months she spent in a Chinese internment camp in India that changed her life forever. I could sense the loss she felt whenever she spoke of her father, who, though still alive at the time, would never again be the father she had in India.

In March 1997, my mother and I spent a week travelling in a camper through the beautiful desert terrain of Death

Valley in California. One evening we joined fellow stargazers for a full lunar eclipse, which darkened the sky momentarily, so we could more clearly see the infamous and bright Hale-Bopp Comet. Like the sky, mother and daughter's timing seemed to be perfectly aligned: I was enrolled at the time in an oral history course and was hungry to understand my family history. Simultaneously, my mother felt enough time had passed to allow her to explore the painful memories that had led to the dissolution of the family of her childhood. This road trip was pivotal in the growth of our relationship, and also a catalyst for her to share the stories you are about to read.

From the first time she mentioned her complicated history and the months she spent in a Chinese internment camp in India, I felt a deep gnawing for greater understanding. As she shared her memories more freely, following our desert road trip, new questions surfaced. Eager to weave her stories, our family history, and this history together within a larger context, I decided to write my bachelor's thesis on the 1962 China–India Border War and the internment of Chinese Indians. Since this history is largely undocumented, I relied heavily on interviews with my grandfather, Chi-Pei Hsueh, and mother. Through this process, I more fully understood the impact that this war and ethnic divisions had on our family.

Over the past 15 years, my mother's reluctance to discuss her past has turned into a burning desire to share her story in order that others may learn this history. This growing need to be a witness to the past paralleled my own increasing curiosity about and exploration into our family's history. Our mutual interest brought us closer, and for this I am more grateful than I think she realizes. I have always admired my mother's quiet strength and perceptiveness. Today, I am in awe of her courage and determination to tell this story. I'm proud that she realized how important it was that she do this, that she was willing to write, to make herself vulnerable by sharing her stories.

When people in the United States learn about the Chinese internment camp in India, they immediately make a comparison with Japanese–American internment, though that was on a much larger scale. It took 46 years for the U.S. government to apologize and offer reparations to the Japanese–American community. The Chinese–Indian community—both within India's borders and beyond—is still waiting for an apology from the Indian government and the relief of validation that comes with acknowledgement of wrongdoing.

My mother's relationship with India is bittersweet. On the one hand, the country forced her out, and on the other, it will always be her home. She has always identified strongly with her Chinese cultural roots—perhaps even more so because of this experience—but only recently have I noticed her also proudly embracing her Indian cultural heritage as well.

The imprisonment of Chinese Indians from 1962–1965 is another example of how political circumstances can create divisions and tension along ethnic lines, forever changing the lives of the individuals involved. There are countless examples—past and present—of ethnic, religious, racial and other identifiable differences dividing families, communities and nations.

Before embarking on this storytelling journey, my mother told me it was important that she not emphasize her struggle in negative terms. Rather, she wanted her story to help educate others on the danger of creating divisions along ethnic and racial lines, and how this can impact families and communities. She wanted her memoir not to serve as material for further division, but to inspire greater understanding.

It took my mother fifty years to tell her story. Now, on the 50th anniversary of the China–India Border War and Chinese internment in India—and with the timely publishing of this memoir—my mother seems more at peace than ever and complete in her identity. She is, all at once, Chinese, American, and Indian.

Nicole Yuin Marsh
June 10, 2012

Prologue

It was a historic moment; after all, it had been forty years since I had left India. I pulled out my camera and was one of the first off the plane. I wanted photos of my family as they disembarked. As the passengers came off the plane, we were told to queue up on the tarmac and wait for an escort into the terminal. Suddenly, a man appeared in front of me. Middle-aged, mustached, and wearing a light khaki uniform. He approached me with such authority, I was sure he was an airport official but his manner was overtly aggressive and far from welcoming.

"What is your name?" He asked. "Your camera," he gestured while reaching out for my camera. "Give me your camera. I want you to give me your camera!"

"What? Why do you want my camera?" I resisted, holding onto it tightly.

"Don't you know that it is forbidden to take any photos at the airport? Now, give me your camera!"

I was astounded.

"I'm sorry," I said, "but I didn't know that it was forbidden. I only took two photos of my family as they came off the plane. All the other photos in the camera were taken in other places, not here in India."

He insisted that I hand it over, but I held on to it. We argued. Finally, realizing that I wasn't going to give up my camera easily, he looked at me sternly and asked: "Your name, what is your name?" I reluctantly gave it to him. "I will be waiting for you inside the terminal." Then he disappeared just as quickly as he had appeared.

I suddenly began shaking, then sobbing, completely out of character to any one who knows me. Why did I have to come back to India? What a stupid thing to have done. Why is it that I was the only one that was targeted? (At the time, it did not occur to me that perhaps it was because I was the only one to whip out my camera and start taking pictures at the airport.) Thank goodness I had my children around me. I held my daughter's hand tightly as the line of people made its way into the terminal. Slowly, I stopped shaking, gathered myself, and prepared for a hard battle with the official—but he never came back. Apparently, this sort of incident is not uncommon.

When I was last in India, the place of my birth, it was 1962. For most Americans, that year was a watershed when the United States and the Soviet Union were on the brink of a Third World War over the Cuban Missile Crisis. But those events were far away from me. I was a shy 13-year-old girl of Chinese descent living in Darjeeling, India, with my enterprising parents who ran a popular restaurant. Then, in October, India and China went to war over a long-simmering border dispute, known as the Sino-Indian Border War.

Darjeeling was a remote outpost, beyond India's more intense urban centres, idyllically situated in the foothills of the Himalayan mountains and known for its famous tea and as a place for explorers to gather before scaling the mountains. I had spent most of my life in the sheltered and confined environment of a convent boarding school. The war shattered my protected world and catapulted me into a chaotic one. I was forced to make decisions that would have irrevocable and lasting consequences when my father was suddenly arrested, held without ever being charged of anything, and then put in prison. We had no idea why. Soon other Chinese nationals were picked up and disappeared strangely out of sight of their friends and neighbours.

As my mother was away, developing new business opportunities in Nepal, I became solely responsible for my elderly grandmother and eight-year-old brother. The month after my father was arrested was the longest month of my life. After only a few weeks, we were finally reunited with him, but this reunion took place in the Darjeeling jail where the four of us, along with hundreds of other Chinese, were placed for a few days, then loaded onto a train, and transported over a thousand miles across India to an internment camp in the remote Rajasthan desert. Several months later, my brother and I were the first two lucky prisoners to be freed. Many remaining internees, however, were forced to languish in the camp for over five years, during which time they lost property and businesses, and saw the break-up of their families, and the disappointment of being abandoned by former friends and colleagues. In all, over 2,500 were held without charge, without due process, and without any guilt other than being ethnically Chinese.

This period may have been a small portion of my life in terms of years, yet it left a huge scar. Most significantly, it led to the disintegration of my family. For the most part, I successfully filed those events deep in my memory and moved on with my life. I had come to America with my mother, her new husband, and my brother, started anew, and never talked about this period of my life to anyone. It wasn't until just over ten years ago that I began to open this chapter of my childhood beyond my immediate family and thus initiated the healing process.

In January 2001, my husband (a retired foreign service officer) and I had been living in Berkeley, California, for many years; we had raised two children who were no longer living at home. My older sister, living in Virginia, phoned me excitedly. Her best friend's daughter was getting married and she invited me to accompany her to the wedding in Calcutta. Wow! My mind started racing. I hadn't thought much about returning to India, much less Calcutta, as we used to call the city where we had lived decades ago. Unexpectedly, my thoughts returned to 1962 and revisited what had happened to us, those events that had forced us to leave India, the country of my birth. I had sworn I would never return and blamed the Indian government for breaking up our family and for confiscating everything we owned. I had so much anger I never wanted to have anything to do with that part of my life again.

It had been my sister's good fortune to escape the Sino-Indian War period. Quite a few years older than I, she was away, attending college in the United States. So when she asked me to accompany her to India, a trip that held only excitement for her, it took me an interminable amount of time to decide whether or not I would go back. After deliberation and indecision, I finally decided to go and was even starting to pleasantly anticipate the prospect of seeing my native land again. Then, while preparing for the trip, an incident rekindled my nascent anxiety.

My husband accompanied me to the Indian Consulate in San Francisco to apply for my visa in late October of 2000. When we arrived, we saw a long line of applicants winding through a narrow hallway that curved towards the visa window. We joined the line and began to inch our way forward. We waited for about two hours as more people arrived and the line began to extend out the door. Most of the applicants were Indian expatriates returning to their homeland for vacation, family or business trips. Some were applying for visas, while others were arriving to pick up completed paperwork. As the hallway grew more thickly crowded, people began to push and shove and it got hot and stuffy. The officious clerks were so slow and bureaucratic; several people lost their tempers. Suddenly, I grew dizzy and nauseous. I told my husband I needed fresh air and was going to go outside; I requested that he call me when he got to the window. He was perplexed as he had never seen me in such a state in all the 30 years we had been married. I felt I was making a big mistake by returning to India.

Nevertheless, we persevered, acquired the visas, and two months later, our plane touched down on the runway at Dumdum Airport in Calcutta. Originally, there were only four of us planning to make the trip but, in the end, our number grew to ten. My sister, her friend, our father and his second wife were already waiting for us in Calcutta, having travelled there from various locations. The six people in our group included my son and daughter—both in their mid-twenties—my brother, his friend, and his fifteen-year-old daughter. (My own mother had passed away years ago.) It had been forty years since we were all reunited in India. I was thrilled to finally be returning to my home when I encountered the airport official trying to intimidate me into giving up my camera.

Ultimately, the Calcutta trip turned out well as we celebrated a four-day Bengali-Punjabi wedding. Unavoidably, the trip was also an emotional one for my family and I. After the festivities, we went to look for the building where my parents and I had lived before moving to Darjeeling; the building was still there, though sorely in need of maintenance. The lift was broken, stuck between the second and third floors; apparently, it had been that way for a decade. We went up to the third floor in the hope of finding someone kind enough to let us in to see our old flat. We knocked on the apartment door and were fortunate to find people at home. A Sikh man opened the door. He was mystified to see so many of us standing there so early in the morning. It was around nine a.m. and he was getting ready to go to work. He still had netting over his beard, as many Sikhs put their beards in a net overnight so that it remains neat and intact the next morning. He greeted us and we apologized for invading his privacy. We told him that we were visiting India after forty years and came by in the hope of viewing the flat where we had once lived. His wife joined him at the door and they kindly invited us in to have a look around and even graciously offered us tea. They were very curious and interested in our story.

Next, our itinerary took us to Darjeeling. My siblings and I wanted to show our kids where we had spent our childhoods. We visited our old apartment building and the restaurant we had once owned. Like the building in Calcutta, the apartment was also run down—in my memory it had once been an elegant building constructed at the time of the British Raj. Although we could not get into our flat (the current owner was away), we could see an old wooden chair in the exterior hallway. My sister became animated as she recognized it as having belonged to our grandmother. The day after our arrival in Darjeeling, I talked everyone (except for my father and stepmother) into hiking down to the jail where we were first imprisoned. At eighty-seven, my father was in poor health and unprepared for the physical or emotional challenge of the jail excursion. For me, it was the most intense experience of the trip.

Our little group gazed down at the prison building and I broke down again in uncontrollable tears. My son held me for several minutes; we both realized for the first time how long I had bottled up my emotions.

Two years after my trip back to India, I experienced another incident in 2003, which compelled me to write this memoir. I had received an email from the only person with whom I had remained in contact from my school days at the Catholic girls' school I attended in Darjeeling, the Loreto Convent. Maureen Blake was from Burma, but her parents had sent her to boarding school in India. I didn't know her well, she was a class ahead of me, and the older girls seldom mingled with younger schoolmates. Then, in one of life's amazing coincidences, a few years after her family emigrated to New

Zealand from Burma, she met and married my husband's cousin, a native of New Zealand. Because of this family connection, we got to know each other and kept in touch. In her email, she informed me about a joint Loreto-North Point alumni reunion in Thailand. North Point was a Jesuit boy's school, considered Loreto's "brother school". Would I attend? she wanted to know. At first I said no. Did I really want to go back and meet schoolmates I hadn't been in touch with after all these years? So many friendships had abruptly ended when our school closed early at the outbreak of the war; everyone was sent home. Forty years is a long time. Again, I debated for weeks whether to go or not; in the end, Maureen and I both decided to attend the reunion with our spouses. She and her husband flew to Thailand from New Zealand, while we flew there from San Francisco.

The reunion was most enjoyable. It had been so long since I had met anyone who had attended the same school and it was fun to meet and talk with people who had shared similar school memories. I introduced myself to one North Point alumnus and told him where we used to live. I mentioned that my family had owned Park Restaurant. He told me his name was Eric and after we talked a bit, he looked at me—curiously at first—and then excitedly: "I know you," he said, "We lived in the same building! What happened to you people? One day you were there, and the next day you were gone. Where did you all go?"

"You don't know what happened to us?" I asked in disbelief.

I told him how our family had all been arrested a month after school closed in October of 1962. I told him about being sent to an internment camp in Rajasthan where my brother and I were held for two-and-a-half months and my father was interned for fifteen months. Eric was flabbergasted. I described how after we were released from the camp, we were not allowed to return to Darjeeling and had lost all our property. It was the first time he had ever heard anything about that.

The subject of the 1962 Border War came up again in another conversation, this time with a woman from Dubai who came with her husband, an alumnus of North Point. As a history teacher, she knew something of the war in general, but when I mentioned the internment camp, she was just as shocked as Eric had been. She had never learned about this. Everyone with whom I spoke and shared my story had the same reaction. No one knew about the internment of the Chinese Indians during the Sino-Indian War.

When I returned home to the United States, I became emboldened to talk about the 1962 Border War and what had happened to my own family. That war and its consequences were pivotal for so many of us. It caused life to change forever. Yet, few people know about it, while fewer still have heard of the internment of ethnic Chinese in India as a result of the war's tensions. I decided it was my obligation to record all that I could remember and tell my story.

Most of what I can share is from memories acquired when I was a child of thirteen; I only cover those years of my life and have pieced together vignettes gathered from interviews and snippets of conversations with my father when I visited him over the years. My father, like my mother and sister, also ended up living in America. He began a new family, too, but like me, he was reluctant to talk about that time in our lives.

When I began to write this memoir, my father had just passed away. Fortunately, my daughter had completed her college senior thesis in 1998 on the "Chinese Internment in India" which she had based on oral histories with her grandfather and me. In the spring of that year, she had interviewed my father by phone and he told her many interesting stories that I have woven into my own memoir.

1

Chungking to Calcutta

My father was born in China in the area once known as Sikang. "Kham", as my father preferred to call his homeland, was an autonomous region in Western China bordering Tibet. After the Communists took control of China in 1949, Sikang became incorporated into the Province of Szechwan. My father grew up in the city of Kangding and was brought up mainly by his mother and an older sister. His father was the district judge who spent most of his time on the road resolving conflicts or problems among the people in his district. Besides attending his regular school, my father was enrolled in a missionary school for several hours each week where he learned to speak English. He became good friends with the English missionary and learned about England and English history. When the missionary returned home, he left my father his dictionary, which became his most treasured possession. At age fourteen, he was sent to Chengdu in Szechwan to attend high school. After he graduated in 1932, he travelled far from home to Central China, to attend

Nanking University. Although he studied Political Science, his true love was Chinese history.

My mother was born in Central China in the city of Yang Chou, famous for its beautiful women. Yang Chou is about fifty miles from Nanking. When she finished high school, her father allowed her to go to Nanking to attend nursing school, but forbade her to visit Shanghai—the "sin city" which was a metropolis full of excitement, danger, and many foreigners. Shanghai is about one hundred and eighty miles from Nanking. She obeyed her father's orders and remained in Nanking after graduating and found a job in the main hospital. Not long after she began her new job, a close friend of my father's, also from Kham, was admitted to the hospital and my mother was assigned to be his attending nurse. He became enamoured with her but since he was already married, he introduced her to his best friend, my father. Several months later my father proposed and my parents were married in 1937. They had planned to stay on in Nanking but their plans were thwarted by the invasion of China by Japan.

When the Nationalist Party overthrew the Ching Dynasty in 1911 and ended thousands of years of Imperial rule, it wanted to cut off all previous ties with the Imperial Court. They wanted a "clean" break, so they moved the capital from Peking to Nanking. When Japan invaded China, one of its first goals was to occupy Nanking. It did so in a horrific invasion where at least 300,000 Chinese were massacred and thousands more fled the city to avoid death. Many who fled joined the Kuomintang (KMT) army, including my parents. When the KMT lost Nanking to the Japanese, the government retreated to Chungking, which became the wartime capital.

After several years of military service, my parents were honourably discharged. My father immediately went to work for Bao Yuan Tung Trading Company in Chungking, which was in partnership with Lever Brothers of England. My parents were grateful for this new start in civilian life and my mother looked forward to staying home and looking after their young daughter, my older sister. My father did well at the company and when the managing director found out that he could speak English, he asked him to relocate to India to take over the management of the Calcutta branch, which was not doing well. He was elated to accept this offer because it gave him the opportunity to see another country. It was a good time to leave China while the Sino-Japanese War was still raging, and while China was in the midst of its own civil war.

The only practical way to get to India under wartime conditions was to travel overland and since my father still had connections in the Nationalist army he was able to obtain safe passage through the war zones. In return, he agreed to serve as an undercover wartime correspondent and provide the Nationalists with intelligence on Communist troop movements and other activities that he might observe during his travels. My parents decided it was best that he go first; my mother and four-year-old sister would join him after he settled down. My father's journey to India started in Chungking and continued southwest through Yunnan Province into Burma, following the Burma Road. He used whatever mode of transportation he could find, including donkey carts. He arrived in Calcutta in 1944, several months after setting out, and immediately assumed his duties as the new manager of the Bao Yuan Tung Trading Company. Years later, whenever he spoke about his import business, he was always animated: he loved his work and his new life in India. As a gregarious and sympathetic manager, he was well liked and was able to turn the company around rapidly.

One of the major products the company exported to China was jute. Grown mainly in Bengal, jute had become a popular export due to its high quality and uniqueness as a manufacturing fibre: it was soft and pliable, but at the same time, very strong. Prior to exporting jute, the company had transported rice in cotton sacks, which often burst, losing large amounts of grain in each shipment. My father described how sacks were hauled up by dockworkers using baling hooks and how the rice leaked out from holes punctured by the hooks. In the jute sacks, the holes closed up immediately due to the fibre's pliable nature, dramatically reducing the loss of rice. Jute became highly prized and was the mainstay of my father's export business. Among the many products my father's company exported from China into India was silk, which was used to make beautiful Indian saris. He also traded Rolex and Omega watches and Parker fountain pens, items that were status symbols and greatly sought after. In the two years after he took over the management in Calcutta, the company opened a second branch in Dacca and a third in Bombay. My father decided it was time to send for his wife and their now six-year-old daughter.

2

Calcutta

My mother and sister arrived in Calcutta in 1946. Everything was foreign to them. They didn't speak Bengali or English—the official language under British rule. The customs, religion and food were vastly different from what they knew in China and they soon realized they had to adapt to a new life and country as quickly as they could. It did not take long for my mother to realize that business and daily communication—especially for expatriates—was conducted in English, so she started taking English classes.

India was still under British rule but the movement for independence was steadily growing. Muslim leaders were growing suspicious of the Hindu majority in the Indian National Congress and demanded that India be divided into two countries, one for Hindus, and the other for Muslims. During this period of political bargaining, there were violent clashes between the Hindus and Muslims and many lives were lost on both sides. Britain eventually acceded to the idea that the only solution to stop the violence was to create two countries. When India gained independence in 1947, Pakistan was born.

A story my mother shared with me many years later about her first arrival in India during this period of social unrest was how it impacted her personally. It was the first time she had witnessed the intense hatred between Muslims and Hindus. Our family lived on the top floor of a three-story building on Mission Row Extension. (The name was later changed to Ganesh Chandra Avenue.) On a late afternoon, she heard a great deal of commotion in the street so she went out to the balcony to see what was happening. In the distance she saw smoke in many parts of the city and groups of people, mostly men, running in different directions. As she watched the pandemonium, she spotted an overweight man sitting cross-legged on the curb near the intersection, quietly minding his own business. Seconds later, another man appeared, brandishing a big sword. Without slowing his pace, he ran it through the belly of the seated man. She saw his guts fall out onto the street. Immediately, she stepped back into the house from the balcony, faint and sickened by what she had witnessed. As she headed toward the bathroom, she heard banging on the front door and the voice of a man desperately pleading for help. She had hardly been able to absorb what she had just witnessed, so she hesitated. The banging and pleading continued.

Finally, she went to the door. "Who is it?" she asked practising her newly acquired English.

"Memsahib, please, please let me in. I beg of you to let me in."

"I don't know who you are. I'm sorry I cannot let you in. I

am from China. I have only just arrived in India. I don't know what's going on."

"Please, Memsahib, please, let me in. They're going to kill me."

"I don't understand. Who's going to kill you?"

"Memsahib, please. There is a mob of Hindus after me. They want to kill me just because I am Muslim. Please do not send me away to my death."

She felt his desperation. Only minutes before she had witnessed the horrific scene, so she decided to open the door and let him in. She immediately locked it behind him and led him to the far end of the apartment and hid him in a closet in the pantry. Moments later, there was more furious pounding on the door and this time, several angry voices shouting.

"Open the door, open the door!"

She went to the door slowly and repeated what she had uttered earlier in her mixture of Chinese and English. "Who is it? What do you want?"

"Memsahib, we are looking for a man who came running in the direction of this building. This man is very dangerous. He could hurt you or even kill you. We want to help you. Please, let us in and search your house."

"I have not seen anyone all afternoon," replied my mother in a soft but firm voice. "I am Chinese and I just arrived from China. I don't know what is going on. Please go away."

"We must come in and search your house."

"I already told you I have not seen anyone but, in case the man comes by, I will certainly turn him over to you. Is that all right?" she asked in a gentle voice.

Satisfied with her response, they eventually left. She waited for some time. When things quieted down and night had fallen, she went to the stranger and told him it was safe to come out. He couldn't thank her enough for saving his life and quickly left her house. She told us that she often wondered what became of him. She never saw him again.

3

Calcutta Chinese

There have been records on Chinese travelling to India as far back as two hundred and fifty years ago. In the nineteenth century, there were only a handful of Chinese who had emigrated to India. According to censuses taken in Calcutta over the years, the Chinese population in the mid-1800s was around three hundred and increased to about eight hundred towards the end of the century. The number continued to increase steadily during the first half of the twentieth century, and a census taken in the mid-1900s had the Chinese population up to around forty thousand. This increase was influenced by a number of "push-pull" factors. Whenever the Chinese suffered hardships back home they looked to other countries for the chance of a better life. Likewise, when there was political instability, rebels escaped China for fear of their lives. Many fled to India or to other parts of Southeast Asia. Conversely, immigration to India slowed when diplomatic relations between the two countries were strained.

The three major ethnic groups to emigrate from China to India were from the southeastern coastal regions of China: Canton, Fukien, and Hubei. Most of these groups were seafaring and generally more open to travel abroad. The largest number was the Hakka, a group of people within these provinces who had originally migrated south from northern China. Other Chinese groups called them Hakka, meaning, "guest people" because they tended to be clannish. This is probably why their name stuck even after several generations. Most Chinese settled in Calcutta, which had been the centre of commerce for at least two hundred years when the British started trading in India.

The Hakka dominated the tanning industry because it was an undesirable trade among the Hindu population. It was the Hindu belief in the sacredness of the cow that made working with leather products polluting. As a result, this trade was generally non-competitive and the Hakka easily slipped into it. Despite the negative religious view of this trade, along with the relative lack of competition, there was high demand for leather goods and this provided many Chinese with a lucrative way of life.

Cantonese immigrants were often carpenters, while Hubeinese often worked in dental clinics. Other businesses held by the immigrant Chinese, such as shoe shops, hairdressing salons and restaurants, sprang up to support the Chinese community. Of course, these generalizations do not include all Chinese immigrants.

Before 1962, the Indian government and native Indians generally did not resent the Chinese in India. Perhaps because they were willing to work in jobs the Indians didn't want, and since their numbers were so small and they had little political power, they did not present a threat.

When India gained its independence from Britain in 1947, and the Chinese Communists established a new regime in China in 1949, these emerging nations shared a common bond and envisioned a new Asia with a close alliance between the two countries. The next ten years were a honeymoon period between China and India. The popular phrase during that time was "*Hindi Chini Bhai Bhai*" which meant "Indians and Chinese are brothers."

The Indian government was one of the first to recognize the Peoples Republic of China as the new legitimate government, and encouraged Chinese living in India to register for citizenship with the PRC. The honeymoon period was short-lived and soon deteriorated with the increasing tension between the two countries over border territory. This disagreement came to the forefront in the late 1950s and early 1960s, culminating in a border war in 1962. Though the war lasted only a month, the residual effects on the relations between China and India have lasted many decades. Likewise, the Chinese living in India suffered a great deal as a result of this conflict. The steady increase of Chinese immigration came to a halt because of the deteriorating relationship between the two governments, and the Chinese began to emigrate from India to seek stability and a home elsewhere.

4

My Family

My parents were different from most of the Chinese living in Calcutta at this time. While the majority of the Chinese in Calcutta came to India by their own choosing, my parents, on the other hand, were sent to India by their employer. The Calcutta Chinese were from coastal provinces but my father was from the hinterland of Western China bordering Tibet, and my mother, from central China.

My father also looked different. He was 5' 10", a head taller than the average Chinese, had curly hair, and spoke Mandarin, along with his native dialect of Kham. He was sympathetic and charmed both his customers and friends. He was a good athlete, played competitive tennis at the gymkhana club, and had been an excellent horseman since childhood. He was called Chi Pei Hsueh and was a wonderful storyteller. I discovered this later when I got to know him as a thirteen-year old, but there were two things I remembered about him from my childhood. The first thing I remembered was that he sang me to sleep every night with his version of Bing Crosby's

"Lullaby". When he was away on business trips, my mother had to put on Bing Crosby records as a backup; otherwise, I would not go to sleep.

The second thing was that he would happily carry me on his back when we went out for walks. I had difficulty keeping up with him on the steep Darjeeling paths and only had to whine, "Papa, my leg's hurting. I can't walk any more! Carry me!" and he would pick me up. We often passed the rickshaw stand where we stopped and visited with the two or three rickshaw pullers that were present. They were Khamba from his native land, and were always happy to see my father. They had animated conversations in their native tongue, a Tibetan dialect, and neither my mother nor I understood them. On one of our visits, I saw a Tibetan terrier puppy peeking from under one of the rickshaw pullers' blankets. It was so cute and fluffy; I immediately fell in love with it. I pleaded with my father if I could take it home, to which he replied that it belonged to the rickshaw puller who loved it too. I reluctantly accepted that, but insisted we pass by the stand at every opportunity so that I could play with the puppy. A few months later, on my birthday, I received a big box and, lo and behold, in it was the little brown Tibetan terrier. My parents had bought the puppy from the rickshaw puller. The previous owner had called him Lhasa but we later changed Lhasa to Lassie, after the popular movie.

My mother was also different from the Calcutta Chinese women. She too was taller than the average Southern Chinese woman. Her name was Hsu Chou and, like my father, she spoke Mandarin, and her native Yang Chou dialect. Neither of them spoke Cantonese, Fukinese, or any of the mainstream dialects spoken by the Calcutta Chinese. She was a beautiful, warm, and compassionate person, admired for her strength and fairness. She had a way with people, and her staff were always happy to work for her. They became loyal employees. Beneath her beauty and elegance, however, she was tough; she took no nonsense from anyone and was never shy about telling you how she felt about anything. She made most of the decisions concerning her children and the household. We loved her immensely and were scared to death of offending her. My parents were a handsome couple. They had an active social life because of their business connections and regularly took part in local amateur Chinese opera and theatre for fundraising events.

My mother became more involved in the trading business as it was winding down, and when my parents started their new restaurant business in Darjeeling, she worked alongside my father and had a bigger role in decision-making. Much later, after my sister left home, my mother became more independent, travelling to Nepal on her own to investigate business opportunities there. In 1960 she opened one of the first beauty salons in Kathmandu. A year later, she opened a hotel, which included a beauty shop and the first Chinese restaurant. She never returned to India.

My grandmother, my mother's mother, left China in late 1948 to join our family in India. We called her Popo. The Communists were getting more and more of a foothold in China, and life for Popo grew more difficult. Her husband was a general in the Nationalist army and was away a great deal fighting the Japanese. Whenever he had leave, he preferred spending it with his mistress. Popo became increasingly depressed and more isolated in China. Her children were scattered: one was overseas in India; two were in the army, and two at the university. My mother believed that if Popo came to India her life would be happier. She explained to her that both she and my father were busy with their business and would be grateful if she came to India to help raise the children and manage the household. Popo finally agreed and arrived in Calcutta a few months before I was born, just as China closed its doors to the outside world.

Popo immediately took over the responsibility of raising me and then my brother, especially during our pre-school years. She became a big part of our lives. Later, when I was sent to boarding school and returned home for holidays, she would look at me and say, "Aiya, kuai kuai, you are so skinny! What are they feeding you in school?" She always tried to fatten me up before I went back to school. She did most of the cooking at home and we loved her food.

I'm not sure how old Popo was when she first came to live with us. She was always seventy-one to me, but she probably was much younger than I thought. Our parents never talked about anyone's age and we never asked. I don't know what her birth name was. We just knew her as Popo. She was born in Yang Chou during the era when foot-binding was still practised in China. She was probably one of the last people of her generation to have her feet bound and it inhibited her from doing many things. Walking any distance, something most of us take for granted, was difficult for her and she was unable to stray too far from the house because her small feet would begin to ache and tire quickly. She often carried her *mora*—a portable stool—with her when she went on walks. When she got tired, she would find a quiet spot and sit on it to rest until she could move on again. Her mora was made from bamboo and hemp rope, and the round seat was fashioned out of animal skin. It was about fifteen inches high.

When we lived in the big city of Calcutta, Popo occasionally got lost. She had no sense of direction. Every time before she went out for her afternoon stroll, my parents would remind her to walk up to a landmark they had picked out, then reverse her steps to return home. They advised her not to make any turns. For the most part she did what she was told but at times she got distracted and forgot, or just made a turn and got terribly lost. My mother would panic when Popo did not return at the expected time; she would then send the servants out to look for her.

As young children, our parents didn't talk about the custom of foot-binding or about Chinese culture in general. We just accepted the fact that Popo had tiny feet. I remember seeing my grandmother unbind her feet only once, but seeing the complicated procedure was enough for a lifetime. It happened when I was home for the holidays, and sleeping in Popo's room. I was nine. I had just woken from a nice sleep and noticed Popo sitting on her favourite chair. She was in the process of unbinding her feet. On the floor beside her feet, was an enamel basin of hot water. I was fascinated because I had never seen her do this before.

"Popo, what are you doing?"

"I am taking care of my feet because they have been giving me a lot of discomfort lately."

"Why, what's wrong? What did you put in the water?" I asked. "Boric acid. It helps soothe my feet."

I watched her take all the cloth binding off her feet, which seemed like yards and yards of narrow cloth. She then sprinkled some white powder into the basin and put her feet in it. There was such an expression of relief on her face. Then I looked down at her feet, the first time I had ever seen them bare. I was shocked. They were so small, the size of a clenched fist. Her feet had been broken when she was a young child so that the top portion of her feet, including her toes, folded under the rest of her feet. She told me calluses formed under her feet and this caused her pain and discomfort; every now and then, she had to use a razor blade to shave them away. She said the hot water and the boric acid softened the calluses and made them easier to shave off. Tears welled up in my eyes. I had no idea how much she had suffered all her life and I began to feel guilty about all the times we were naughty and deliberately made her chase us because we knew she could never catch us.

Popo looked at me and said, "Don't be sad, kuai, kuai. I am used to this now. I've lived with it all my life. But, the best thing that happened for me was when your great-grandfather forbade this ritual to be performed on your mother. She never had to face my fate."

Popo continued, "In the past, a young woman of decent birth often could not find a husband if she didn't have bound feet."

"Popo, that is so terrible! How did this custom get started?" I asked her but she wasn't able to answer me. I couldn't imagine why in ancient times, Chinese men found women with bound feet so attractive. How could women be subjected to such cruelty? I thought it was so wicked and I was glad I wasn't born any earlier.

My sister was born in China in 1940 when the Sino-Japanese War was in full force; at the same time the Chinese people were waging their own bitter civil war. My grandfather, a general in Chiang Kai-Shek's army, experienced the war firsthand. He said that a child born into this dark chaos should give people hope for "Universal Brightness" so he named her Pu-Chin.

As a child, I didn't call my sister by her name. I called her Gigi. The word for big sister in Chinese is Jie Jie, and the word for sister in Hindi, is Di Di. When adults talked about her to me they would say one or the other depending on whether they were Chinese or Indian and, most likely, I combined the two words and called her Gigi. She was someone we looked up to. She was always the "big sister" who had already experienced everything. We saw each other mostly during winter break; when she was not busy with her own friends, she would take me on many adventurous outings. Like my parents, she was a great storyteller and was a lot of fun. Unfortunately, our years together were curtailed by the fact that she was away in boarding school when I was born. When I grew older I was also sent off to boarding school. We overlapped for three years but saw little of each other in school since she was nine years older and in the upper division. I was eight and a half when she left home to attend university.

In a recent conversation, I asked Pu-Chin how she ended up in boarding school in Darjeeling, instead of Calcutta. She told me that soon after she and our mother arrived in India, she was enrolled in a local school in Calcutta that taught English. Our parents had tried to enroll her in the best English school in Calcutta but it had a long waiting list. Towards the end of 1949, after Pu-Chin had turned nine, Mother Superior at the

Catholic day school in Calcutta informed my parents that she was being transferred to Loreto Convent in Darjeeling, which had the reputation of being the best girls' school in the country. There were openings and she encouraged my parents to enroll my sister there. She reassured them that she would watch out for her. My parents agreed it was the best option, so Pu-Chin was sent to Darjeeling the following March.

I came into this world the same year China fell to the Communists. Our family became stateless by choice since both of my parents refused to accept the new Communist regime. They chose not to register as Chinese citizens in India, nor did they want to return to China under Mao Tse-Tung. They chose to make India their home permanently. Since the world was in chaos, my father named me Yin-Chin, "yearning for brightness." My mother used to tell me that as a young child, I was gregarious, curious and full of humour. I think I lost all that after years in boarding school.

My brother was born in 1954 when I was four. My father named him Yuin Kieng, to be "forever strong." He was the first boy in the family and was affectionately called Bao Bei, "little treasure." Bao Bei gradually morphed into Bobby, which is how people know him today. He and I didn't interact much the first few years of our lives since I was at boarding school. It wasn't until 1960 when we both visited our mother in Nepal during our three-month winter holiday that we started to know each other. He was six and I was ten. We spent two consecutive winters with her, which cemented our relationship.

Although not related to our family, two important people in my life were Borjee, our cook, and Ayah, our nanny. I don't

Front: Ta-Tung Chou (cousin), Popo with Bobby, Yin-Chin Back: Pu-Chin,
Chi Pei Hsueh (Papa), Hsu Chou (Mother) (1954 Calcutta)

know if Borjee means cook or whether it was his real name.
We just called him Borjee. He was from Madras in Southern
India and migrated to Calcutta for work. My parents were
looking for a driver and during the interview with my parents,
he told them he didn't drive but that he had some experience
as a cook. My mother liked him immediately and hired him
on the spot. He became our family cook and my mother
taught him to make Chinese food. A quick learner, he soon
took over the marketing and planning of the meals. Later,

when my parents went into the restaurant business, they took Borjee to Darjeeling and he became the main chef at Park Restaurant. He was excellent in both Indian and Chinese cuisine. By the time I was born, he was already a part of the family and became one of my favourite people.

Later, when I made my monthly weekend visits home from school, I took the southern route because I passed Park Restaurant on the way. I usually went to say hello to Borjee in the kitchen before I went to see my parents. He would give me a snack or just say, "You're home, chota baby. Good to see you, but you are so thin!" I knew if he said that, Popo was bound to say the same thing. If he happened to be preparing the spices for the Indian meals that day, I would stay and watch him. He placed the various spices on his flat stone mortar, then used his pestle to grind the seeds into powder. His mortar was a large flat black stone about nine inches wide, twelve inches long and two inches thick, and weighed a ton. His pestle was also a heavy black stone three inches in diameter and six inches long. Other times, when I caught him in the middle of lunch, I would simply squat near him and chat and tell him everything I did in school. He would also clue me into the goings-on in the restaurant. I loved watching him eat because he made the food look so delicious. My family ate with chopsticks and I learned to use a knife and fork in school. Borjee ate with his fingers. He mixed his curry and rice to form a ball and then shoved it into his mouth. He would then take a bite of a large, very hot green chili. He had a chili with every meal and since he was from Madras, he had no problem handling extremely spicy food. He called my sister baby, but when I was born, he started calling her "bara baby" (big baby) and me "chota baby" (small baby.)

Borjee let me play in the restaurant chicken coop even though he wasn't supposed to. He knew how I loved chasing chickens. The restaurant's huge coop held twenty or thirty chickens. It must have been around 200 square feet on a sloped dirt ground. Whenever my father bought chickens from the market, he would have them delivered to the restaurant and Borjee supervised their release into the coop. During the day the chickens were let out into the large caged area where they foraged; at night, they were shooed into a securer area. There were many jackals in Darjeeling and the cooks were not about to lose any chickens.

One day, when I came home from school, Borjee showed me his new pet: a big, beautiful, red rooster that he had raised from a chick. It was an amazing bird, more like a dog than a rooster. He called him Red and it followed him everywhere. It came when he called it and even protected Borjee when people teased him. The kitchen staff, or friends of theirs, couldn't believe a rooster would protect its master so they often pretended to chase or harm Borjee to see how Red would react. When they did this, the rooster would start clucking aggressively and chase after them. I was always a little scared of Red because of his huge claws but as long as Borjee was present it was safe.

One day the rooster attacked and injured a new staff member of the restaurant who had teased Borjee relentlessly. The man took revenge when Borjee was away one day: he caught and killed big Red. When Borjee found out later, he was enraged; he probably would have killed the man if others had not intervened. It was like losing a son. Borjee threatened to quit as long as this man still worked in the restaurant. Eventually, my mother intervened. She was not about to lose her most valuable employee who was like a member of the family so she fired the "rooster killer". Borjee was depressed for months after that incident and I had never seen him so sad.

The other very important person in my childhood who was not a member of my family was Ayah. Her real name was Kirin Bala Das, a Bengali from Dacca, East Bengal (before India's independence). Because she was Hindu, she was forced to migrate to Calcutta during the "Great Migration" of India in 1947 when India was divided and East Bengal became part of Muslim Pakistan. My mother hired Kirin as a nanny to help my grandmother after Bobby was born. We called her Ayah, which means nanny in Hindi. She was a diminutive woman and always wore saris.

Ayah looked after Bobby as if he were her own son. When our family moved to Darjeeling, Ayah came with us. Much later, when my mother went to Nepal, she sent for both Ayah and Borjee to join her. Ayah helped my mother in her beauty salon and Borjee became the chef in her hotel. Both Borjee and Ayah worked for us until we left the subcontinent. Then, Borjee returned to his home city of Madras; Kirin stayed on in Kathmandu and opened her own hairdressing salon.

5

Darjeeling

When the Communist Party took control of China, it took over all privately-owned businesses and started taking over all foreign subsidiaries as well. My father was contacted and told that he was now working for the new government which called the country the People's Republic of China. He fought to keep control of his business but lost in the end. He could not find a way to work for the regime he despised and so he resigned. Overnight, he went from being a successful businessman to becoming a person without a country and without work. He was devastated.

The loss affected my father greatly. He became severely depressed which began affecting life at home. My mother's health suffered. She found it difficult to cope with my father's emotional state but also found it increasingly hard to cope with the oppressive heat in Calcutta. They decided they needed a drastic change. They learned of a Chinese restaurant in Darjeeling that was for sale and they were eager to take on the challenge of doing something entirely different. Its year-round cool climate would suit my mother. This was also where my sister Pu-Chin was attending boarding school, which meant she could come home one weekend every month. My parents concluded that this change would be the answer to their problems.

The family moved to Darjeeling shortly after Bobby was born. The distance between Calcutta, at sea level in the plains, and Darjeeling, at the foothills of the Himalayas, is around three hundred miles but the journey was quite arduous and time-consuming due to steep terrain and minimal infrastructure. Typically, it would take two days: first, an overnight train from Calcutta to Siliguri, the last big city in the plains. Then, from Siliguri, there were two choices for making the ascent to Darjeeling: one choice was to hire a taxi—the faster way—which took three hours on a narrow switchback road; the other choice was to take the two-foot, narrow-gauge steam train, a painstakingly slow trip that took up to eight hours. Although the formal name for this train was the "Darjeeling Himalayan Railway", local residents affectionately called it the "Toy Train" because it was so small that it looked like a toy train. (Today it remains as one of a handful of narrow-gauge steam trains left in the world and was added onto the World Heritage List in 1999.)

Our family usually took the car route to and from Calcutta because it was a much shorter trip. I never got used to riding in cars, particularly on winding mountain roads and invariably got carsick. (To this day, I still get carsick travelling in the mountains and always end up driving.) When Bobby got older and travelled with us to Calcutta, he also got carsick and we fought over who got a window seat.

On the rare occasions when we took Lassie, even he couldn't stomach the hairpin turns. Our parents would ask the driver to stop the car several times on the journey so that the three of us could get out and throw up. They felt sorry for us and tried to accommodate us by taking the toy train whenever possible but they preferred travelling by car because it saved so much time.

Toy Train—coming up the mountain

I loved the train even though we got bored at the end of the long day. The scenery was breathtakingly ethereal, trees swaying in and out of the mist, as it was frequently foggy. The mountainside was covered with pine and many species of flora including mountain orchids and timber bamboo. The orchids had tiny, yellow flowers high up in the trees and one could easily miss seeing them. As the large bamboo swayed, one could imagine hearing voices whispering secrets to one another. As we ascended, there were areas where the hillside was so incredibly steep, the train had to slow to a crawl. When this happened, we jumped off the train and ran beside it, then jumped back on when it started to pick up speed. We had so much fun doing this.

My daughter Nikki among the tea bushes, Happy Valley
Tea Estate (2001)

Darjeeling, situated at 6,710 feet with its pure air and temperate climate, became famous during the time of the British Raj in the mid-19th century. The British determined it was the perfect site to establish a sanatorium where soldiers could recuperate. Shortly after the sanatorium was built, Darjeeling was developed into a hill station where British residents living in the plains could escape the heat during the summer months; in 1864 it became the informal summer capital of the Governor of Bengal. The British also discovered that the cool, foggy climate was perfect for tea cultivation and, in due course, Darjeeling, became world famous for its tea.

When I lived in Darjeeling in the 1950s and 60s, the population of about 10,000 included diverse ethnic groups. Although it is in the Indian state of West Bengal, the local inhabitants are ethnically and culturally closer to the people of neighbouring Sikkim, Nepal, and Bhutan than they are to the Bengali people on the plains. The diverse group also included Bengalis who migrated up from the plains, Anglo-Indians, and a smattering of retired British military personnel who had opted to spend the last years of their lives in India rather than return to England. After the Chinese invaded Tibet in 1959, thousands of Tibetan refugees fled to India to escape Chinese persecution. Many settled in the Darjeeling area. In the mix, there were a few Chinese families—ours was one. As a result of this ethnic diversity, there were many languages and dialects spoken in the area. Within my own family, we spoke several languages: my parents and grandmother spoke Mandarin Chinese; my siblings and I spoke English with each other and Chinese with our grandmother. We spoke a mixture of Chinese and English with our parents and Hindi with the servants.

Darjeeling is a very mountainous town. Growing up there, I remember there were two distinct districts: upper and lower. The main bazaar or marketplace was in lower Darjeeling. Upper Darjeeling had boutique shops, upscale restaurants and the hospital. My parents got all the supplies for our home and the restaurant down at the bazaar. I begged them to take me with them when I came home from boarding school for winter break. I loved to watch how my father and mother interacted with the vendors. On occasion my parents would go marketing together, but they usually went separately because they each had special vendors with whom they liked to deal. Each product was allocated to certain areas of the market. For example, dry goods like tea, grain, and spices were concentrated in one section; live poultry was in another; fish

Lower Darjeeling and its market place (2001).

in another; and meat was sold inside a large warehouse with high, arched ceilings. There were about twenty butchers in the building who were always very lively and good-natured. They were either Muslim or Christian, since Hindus were vegetarians. The butchers made their work look like fun as they competed for my parents' business. The fish market was my least favourite—I was repelled by the odour, and always waited outside until my parents moved on to another vendor. Other enterprises like tool and repair shops, small restaurants, and schools were located in lower Darjeeling, including Loreto Convent, the Catholic girls' school and St. Joseph's College, the Jesuit boys' school.

Upper Darjeeling, where we lived, was about six or seven hundred feet above lower Darjeeling. Our family lived in a large yellow apartment building we called Ajit Mansion, built by the British at the end of the 19th century and formerly known as Stephens Mansion. It was only a stone's throw from our restaurant and seconds from Chowrasta, the town plaza.

This open square was probably the only flat space in upper Darjeeling. Its north side was lined with boutique shops and restaurants. The east side had a large pavilion where live concerts took place on Sunday afternoons. There were benches around the square and at the south end of the plaza, opposite Ajit Mansion, were stables. I spent a lot of my time at the stables during holidays since I loved horses and riding. The plaza was a popular place where tourists and locals alike came to sit and relax, shop or eat.

Chowrasta was always on the tourist's "to-do list". Not only because of its many places to shop and eat: it was famous for its view of Mt. Kanchenjunga, at 28,169 feet, the third highest mountain in the world. From here, the majestic mountain looked so close you felt you could just reach out and touch it. Tourists made the long difficult trip to Darjeeling from Calcutta just to see the mountain and often left disappointed at not having seen her at all; the mountain atmosphere was

Mt. Kanchenjunga (mid-1960s).

unpredictable and the peak was often shrouded in fog for days at a time. Local people regarded Kanchenjunga as sacred and it had the reputation of being one of the most difficult mountains to conquer. I always had a special feeling for the mountain: it was "my mountain" and gave me comfort knowing it was always there, so close, majestic, and forever unconquered.

Locals who had businesses around Chowrasta usually lived in upper Darjeeling. Automobiles were generally not allowed in upper Darjeeling because the roads were not designed to handle a large flow of traffic so few residents owned cars and people walked everywhere. As a result, upper Darjeeling always appeared pristine in contrast to the dirty bazaar area where there were many vehicles, primarily long-distance taxis and transport trucks.

When my parents went marketing, they hired coolies to carry our provisions home or to the restaurant. The coolies were usually women who loaded the foodstuff into baskets

My brother Bobby in Chowrasta (2001).

the size of modern-day mountain backpacks. They carried the baskets on their backs and secured them with a wide flat cloth wrapped around their foreheads. I was always amazed at how strong these women were, especially since they had to carry everything uphill. The paths in Darjeeling were very steep and I learned how to walk these pathways by following the coolies who zigzagged instead of going straight up. It was much easier on the legs and lungs.

When my parents took over Park Restaurant and Hotel, they continued to serve Cantonese food but expanded the menu by introducing food from Western and Central China, the regions they were from. There were about half a dozen rooms above the restaurant, which were rented out to visitors and tourists. Park, as the locals called the restaurant, became very popular and was a favorite eating-place for the girls and boys who lived in boarding school and missed home-cooked food. In the boarding schools, the food that was generally served was boiled meats and vegetables, exceedingly bland for those used to eating a variety of spicy and seasoned foods.

Since Park was close to home, we always were in and out of the restaurant. We ate at the restaurant half of the time because that was when we could spend some time with our parents. I loved to go into the restaurant kitchen and bother the cooks, especially Borjee. One of Bobby's and my favourite pastimes was to watch the cooks kill chickens. The cooks would chop off

Darjeeling coolie

their heads and throw the chickens in a pile on the floor. Often the headless chickens would get up and start running about and sometimes would come towards us. When that happened, we would scream in delight and try to get away. It was such a thrill.

Our flat was at the end of a long, wide hallway on the third floor of Ajit Mansion. It faced Chowrasta, with a view overlooking a fountain on the main street where there was always a great deal of activity. People shopped and strolled, met friends or arranged to go riding. We could see the riding stables on the other side of the fountain. The bright and cheery flat was a modest unit with three bedrooms, living-dining room, and a kitchen. When you came through the front door, you entered a small hallway; the kitchen was immediately off to the right and the living-dining room was at the end of the hallway. Popo's bedroom was to the right of the living room with an attached half-bathroom, and our parents' bedroom

Park Restaurant, now the Shangri-La (2001).

was on the left of the living room. These three rooms had bay windows that faced Chowrasta.

Turning left at the door to the living room, you followed another small hallway past the main bathroom on the left, directly opposite my parents' bedroom. Pu-Chin's room was at the end of the hall. Her room, the main bathroom, and the kitchen had windows that faced the exterior corridor. Bobby slept in Popo's room and when I came home on holidays I slept either in Popo's or in my parents' room.

The living room was the busiest room in our house, the centre of everything that took place in our daily lives, and where we ate our meals, entertained guests, read books and listened to the radio. During the winter we had a coal fire every night—the only source of heat. There was a big sofa by the bay window; other chairs and pieces of furniture, including an old Zenith radio lined the walls around the room. Pu-Chin's upright piano sat next to the fireplace. In the

Ajit Mansion. We lived on the top floor with the last three windows.

middle of the room there was a big heavy dining table and chairs, which sat on top of a thick Chinese rug that covered most of the floor.

In front of Ajit Mansion in 2001, with my son, Rex, my niece Jennifer, my 87-year-old father, and me.

6

Loreto Convent

In March of 1954 my parents enrolled me in boarding school. I was four and a half. My parents were given a list of things to bring to school for me that should last from March to November, the entire school year: uniforms, shoes, socks, ties, underwear, cardigans, school blazers, handkerchiefs, essential toiletries, notebooks, pencils, snacks, etc. These were all put in a large black metal trunk, about three feet long and two-feet wide, and a foot high. The trunk accompanied me when they dropped me off in the Assembly Hall, where everyone gathered on arrival day. That first day of school was the most traumatic. It was hard to leave the comfort of home and family and face unknown challenges, new people, and a world of nuns and their strict rules. Many first-year girls, including me, cried our hearts out when our parents finally left us, but with each passing year it became a little easier to say goodbye.

I often wondered why my parents sent me away at such a young age even though my family lived in town. My father used to jokingly tell me that he and my mother found me in a cabbage patch and decided to take me home; for a long time I thought that was why they sent me away. When I was a little older, I questioned my sister about this and she said that was rubbish; she reassured me that our parents did this because they felt we would get better treatment as boarders than as day scholars, the term used to refer to children who lived at home and came to the school each day. Their reasoning was probably well-founded, since my friends who were day scholars told me they were not given the same privileges as boarders; instead, the nuns treated them like second-class citizens. Bobby was luckier than me. He was never put into boarding school. When he was old enough, my parents enrolled him in Bethany School, another Catholic institution, and Ayah walked him to and from school every day.

My school was called Loreto Convent Darjeeling. It was run by the Loreto order of nuns, originally sent to India from Ireland and England in the mid-19th century. Established in 1847, it was one of the first Loreto schools for girls in India and in the intervening years it earned a reputation for being one of the best in the region for its excellent instruction in English. In spite of its remoteness, girls from prominent families all over India and neighbouring countries, including Nepal, Sikkim, Bhutan, Burma and Thailand, were sent to Darjeeling to attend school. We called our school "LCD" for short, which many of us jokingly referred to as "Lunatic Cows Department" or "Lowest Common Denominator". There were around three hundred girls enrolled at school from kindergarten through class eleven. Loreto was primarily a boarding school since two-thirds of the girls were from out of town. "Boarders" arrived early in March and returned home the last week in November after final exams. We had a three-

Loreto Convent

month winter break to allow boarders who had travelled far to return home for longer holidays, but it was also because the winters in Darjeeling were very cold and the school had no central heating. Since I lived in Loreto for nine months of the year, it became my second home.

We had navy-blue and white school uniforms which we wore day in and day out. On weekdays we had to wear a pleated navy-blue skirt with its length just above the knees, a white blouse, a navy-blue cardigan, a striped tie, navy-blue socks, and laced black shoes. On school outings we had to wear a blazer with the school emblem in place of the cardigan, and a navy-blue beret to go along with it. One day a week and on weekends we wore a navy-blue pleated tunic over the white blouse instead of the skirt, and no tie. After I left boarding school I refused to wear anything navy-blue! Not until after graduating from college did I succumb to wearing my first pair of denim jeans.

Since Loreto was a Catholic school, all boarders were required to go to church. Every morning before breakfast and every evening before dinner we had to go to church for prayers. These lasted twenty to thirty minutes. On Sundays we had to attend mass in the morning and benedictions in the evening. These services took considerably longer—up to two or more hours. I wasn't Catholic, but it was one of the requirements of being a boarder. Non-Catholics, however, were not allowed to have communion. I thought it rather unfair since we had to go to church for prayers every day and attend mass every Sunday. I envied the girls who took communion. The host looked like tasty wafers to me and I was curious as to how it really tasted.

My curiosity got the better of me. One day I talked a friend, also a non-Catholic, into sneaking into the priest's vestry to see if we could find any leftover communion wafers. Lo and behold, we didn't expect to find the priest still there. He was quite surprised to see us too and asked us what we were doing there. I had to fess up and told him that we were not Catholics but were curious about communion wafers and wanted to try them. He was very good-natured and told us he happened to have a few that had not been "blessed" and offered one to each of us. We thanked him, put them in our mouths and scampered away as fast as we could. After we reached our dressing rooms, we felt triumphant but decided we hadn't missed much after all. The wafers tasted like cardboard!

The walk from school, below the bazaar, to our home up in Chowrasta wasn't far and probably took thirty to forty minutes to go uphill, but for a young child it seemed to take forever. It was, of course, faster going down. Boarders with families in town were given permission to go home one weekend a month; we were the envy of the other boarders. In the beginning I grumbled a lot about being a boarder, but eventually accepted the fact that I had to live in school since I couldn't convince my parents otherwise. The first two years in boarding school were the hardest. Even though Pu-Chin overlapped with me for three years, she was in the senior division and so busy with her own classes and friends that we didn't see much of each other.

7

The Littlest Outlaw

It took several months before I finally adjusted to living in boarding school. As a newcomer I was sometimes bullied. One morning when we were getting dressed before classes, an older girl began prodding me on the chest. I don't remember why or how it all started. I asked her to stop but she ignored me and kept on prodding. I eventually couldn't take it any more so I returned her prodding with a hard punch and sent her reeling. She screamed and ran to Mrs. Powell saying that I had hit her. Mrs. Powell was the woman in charge of the lower-division girls and took care of organizing the daily rituals of dressing, toiletries, bathing, getting us ready for bed, etc. Without waiting to hear my side of the story, she caught me by the ear, dragged me into a bathroom, and locked me in there.

In school, the toilets, bathtubs, and washbasins were in separate areas. The bathtubs were in private rooms each with a single chair, and the washbasins were in a huge common room with the sinks lined up in two long rows, on opposite walls. These were on the same floor as our dressing rooms. The toilets were on a different floor. We had baths twice a week; each girl was assigned two days of the week for the entire year.

As she locked me inside the bathroom, I protested to Mrs. Powell that it was the other girl who started the fight and that it wasn't fair I was the only one being punished; it was to no avail. I was left alone in the dark bathroom. I banged on the door but was ignored. There was a great deal of commotion outside while the girls were getting dressed and ready for class. It had gotten quiet and when I stopped banging on the door, I realized that everyone had gone off to breakfast. I was angry at first not so much for being punished, but because I felt it was so unjust. A long time passed and I became frightened and started to cry. Still no one came, so I lay on the cold floor and cried myself to sleep. It seemed hours later when the bathroom door finally opened. To my surprise and delight, it was my big sister who had been sent to "release" me. She gave me a big hug and through my sobs I told her what had happened and that I wanted to go home. She comforted me and agreed that I had been wrongly punished. The matter was never mentioned again and the girl who had started it all ignored me after that. Nevertheless, it took me a while to get over the whole incident.

Soon afterwards, I decided I had had enough of living in boarding school and decided to run away. I told my friends what I was planning—most of them didn't believe me, and even tried to dissuade me. They supposed, perhaps correctly, that I could get into trouble, and that they could get into trouble for helping me. Only one friend encouraged me to do it and said she would run away with me when I had it all worked out. Her family lived in town as well. The plan finally came together after we saw a movie. The girls were allowed to watch movies two or three times a year and it was such a big treat, not only for us, but for the nuns as well. The nuns used to get just as excited and animated when it was movie night. The films were always shown in the Assembly Hall. The girls sat on the floor while the nuns sat on the chairs behind us. If there were kissing scenes, one of the nuns would warn us to cover up our eyes. We mostly ignored her. One time, during a kissing scene, a friend whispered, "Hey, look at the nuns." We looked back to where they were sitting and saw that they had covered their eyes but a few had spread their fingers apart. We all giggled at the sight.

The movie that inspired me to run away was called "The Littlest Outlaw". After viewing it, I decided that the time had come to make a plan. "The Littlest Outlaw" was about a boy whose stepfather was a horse trainer who had tried to train a general's horse to jump so that he could enter a competition. The trainer used methods that were so cruel, the horse developed a fear of jumping instead. Whenever the general took the horse out to test its skills, it would come to a dead halt in front of the jumping bar. One time the horse managed to throw the general off its back, which enraged him so much that he gave orders for the horse to be shot. The trainer's son took the horse and ran away with him and became the littlest outlaw.

For days after the movie was shown, I planned my escape. I observed that when the girls were busy in the dressing room getting ready for bed there was a lot of noise and activity and it would be easy to slip away unnoticed. I also observed that no one went into the church after evening prayer. With the help of a couple of other girls, I found out that the main school gate was locked after 6:30 in the evening. The main church door, however, was never locked. I had gone over my plan and the escape route many times and felt I was ready to make a move. On the day I designated for my big escape, I waited until the girls were dismissed from study hall and sent to the dormitory. At the last minute, my fellow escapee changed her mind. I was on my own. I had found a perfect hobo stick a few days earlier to use as part of my runaway gear and had hidden it carefully in a safe place near the school gate.

The shortest route to the school gate was through the church and out its main door. The church was in the shape of a cross. The main body of the cross was for the public and the two arms of the cross were reserved for the schoolgirls. The left side was assigned to the upper-division girls; the right was for the lower division. This was where I prayed every day and attended mass on Sundays along with all the others.

My plan was to enter the wing of the church reserved for the lower-division girls, then pass through the restricted apse where the priests conducted mass. Finally, I would go out through the main body of the church towards the entrance. I had to reach the school gate at the right time because I knew it would be locked after 6:30. On the other hand, if I arrived too early I would face the risk of running into Agnes, the parlour maid, or worse, a nun. (When a girl had visitors, it was one of Agnes' duties to go and look for the girl while the visitors waited in the parlour, or waiting room.) Timing was crucial. I gathered all my precious possessions, bundled them into my headscarf, and then quickly went down from the dormitory hall toward the church.

It was spooky going through the dimly lit church on my own and passing all the statues placed in strategic positions. I was terrified. My heart pounded so loudly I thought somebody would surely hear it and I would get caught. The walls were covered with pictures of saints and other holy people, all staring down at me; there was the ubiquitous scent of incense which added an air of awe and mystery. I made it out without mishap and headed for the gate. My stick was just where I had left it, so I picked it up and tied my bundle onto it, just like I had seen in the movies, swung it over my shoulder and slipped out of the school gates. Once outside, I ran as fast as I could and didn't stop until I arrived at Park Restaurant feeling very pleased with myself, only to face my father's shock when he learned that I had run away from school.

"Yin-Chin, what are you doing here?" he exclaimed.

"I ran away from school and I've come home," I answered, out of breath and very proud of what I had done.

"You're a naughty girl. You can't do that. You must go back right away."

"No, Papa, I won't go back. It took me a long time to plan this."

"You have to go back. The nuns will be very worried when they find out you're missing."

"No, I won't go back!"

My mother intervened and gave me a big hug. "It's wonderful to see you, darling. You should not have run away but that was such a brave thing for you to do. You can spend the night at home and then we will take you back to school in the morning."

Just then Agnes arrived panting. When she saw me, she was relieved she had found me but was very cross at the same time.

"I've come to take Yin-Chin back to school."

"No," I fought back. "I'm not going back to school." I turned and ran out of the restaurant and ran as fast as I could until I reached home and fell into Popo's arms. Popo was so pleased and surprised to see me but didn't question why I was home. In the meantime, my parents persuaded Agnes to return to the convent without me, promising that they would personally take me to school the next day and explain to Mother Superior what had happened. When I was sent back to school the following day, the nun in charge of the lower division scolded me for what I had done, but then softened her tone and explained that I could have gotten lost or harmed by unsavoury people on the way. I was not punished and nothing more was said. I never tried to run away again.

8

Kathmandu

My mother had left India sometime in 1959, about two years after my sister left home. She had gone to Nepal to look for new business opportunities and I missed her terribly. When she was in town, she visited me at school almost every weekend and brought me up to date with the goings-on at home. She always brought me treats and I looked forward to these visits. My father rarely visited me in school when my mother was in town. I used to ask her where Papa was when he didn't show up and she invariably answered, "He's playing tennis." Because tennis had become my competitor for my father's affection, I loathed the game and refused to learn the sport until I was in my mid-twenties. Before my mother left town she came to the convent to tell me she was going to Nepal. She explained that the new restaurant they had opened in Calcutta, the Lighthouse Restaurant, was going well but she was recently offered a wonderful opportunity to visit Kathmandu to see if she could get something started there. She said if she did well she would send word for all of us to join her. I listened to what she had to say and just accepted it and assumed she would return home after a few weeks.

After graduating from Loreto, Pu-Chin was accepted into the University of California at Berkeley. An American couple from Berkeley, who had resided in Darjeeling for a number of years, were frequent customers at Park. They were always happy to visit with my parents with whom they could speak English, and consequently they became close. They liked my sister and knew she had recently graduated from Loreto. They spoke very highly of U.C. Berkeley and encouraged her to apply, promising my parents that they would sponsor her. After she was accepted by the college, and the time came for my sister to leave, my mother accompanied her to Hong Kong; from there, Pu-Chin was on her own for the rest of the journey to a foreign land. It was May of 1957 when my sister left home, four months before I turned nine. I was given special permission to go home and spend the last two days with her. I remember being extremely upset with her for leaving us. America seemed like a different planet, and I was convinced I would never see her again.

At the end of November 1960, school closed for winter holiday and everyone went home. My mother had written to Papa and asked him to send Bobby and me to Nepal to spend the holidays with her. We were so excited. Papa took us to Biratnagar and put us on a plane to Kathmandu. We arrived three hours later and were so happy to see mummy waiting for us on the tarmac. It had been more than a year since we had seen her. She told us it had been hard work but she was successful in getting a new business started; it was going extremely well and she would be ready in another year for us to join her.

Kathmandu was so different from Darjeeling. It was in a beautiful valley about four thousand feet in elevation. The terrain was flat and the temperature was at least twenty degrees warmer in the winter than Darjeeling. It was wonderful for us to walk everywhere without getting winded in our heavy winter clothing. There were very few cars in the city in those days and my mother allowed us to explore the city with at least one member of her staff. There were many temples around the city and we were taken to visit a few. I particularly remember the Hindu Temple at the Pashupatinath River. It was an overwhelming and intimidating place with an incredible confluence of life: people bathing in the holy river, bodies being cremated on its banks and the ashes scattered into it, and sadhus, or holy men, either wandering about temple grounds or meditating. They were awesome to look at with their long beards and long matted hair, naked except for a loincloth. Their bodies were covered in ash, and their foreheads were coloured with yellow and red pigment. Some carried tridents (symbolic of the God Shiva), which made them more frightening. In contrast to this, my world was in a serene and clean environment with Catholic nuns, who were demure and clothed from head to toe.

The other holy place my mother took us to visit was the Buddhist Temple, Bodhnath. She took us once to meet a monk there who was a friend of hers. Bodhnath Temple was not as intimidating as Pashupatinath Temple, but it too had an aura of mystery, with monks sitting cross-legged in the halls of the monastery performing a constant chant. The air was again filled with the combination of incense and smoke of burning candles.

In this first vacation with our mother in Nepal, I got to know her better than I ever had before. She was clever, charming, and compassionate. I found out that she was also a great storyteller. She introduced us to the way she did things. We were in awe of her. She was one of the first women to drive in Nepal, and had her own car brought up from Calcutta. She opened the first Chinese restaurant in Kathmandu, and was the first foreign woman to run a hotel. It was a wonderful three months with our mother, after which we reluctantly returned to Darjeeling in time for the start of the new school year.

The following December, my mother sent for us for another visit. Tempa, her hotel manager in Kathmandu, had asked for leave to visit his wife and family in Darjeeling and had wanted to bring his wife back with him. My mother took this opportunity to ask him to bring us with him too. They lived only about a twenty-minute walk from us.

This time our journey to Kathmandu was exciting and adventurous. We said goodbye to my father and Popo, caught a taxi to Siliguri, then boarded the train to Biratnagar, the largest border town in Nepal, just on the other side of India. We took Lassie with us at my insistence, and somehow got him into our train compartment just in the nick of time. We heard shouts coming from the head of the train and realized the station guard must have seen Lassie being smuggled onto the train. He started heading in our direction, stopping and searching every compartment. I quickly took Lassie onto the top bunk with me and hid him under my blankets and pretended to be asleep. The guard made it to our compartment about ten or fifteen minutes later, and in a gruff and loud voice asked if we had a dog on board. Tempa motioned that he speak quietly since the girl on the top bunk was not feeling well and was asleep, and no, we hadn't seen a dog. We arrived at Biratnagar after a night and a day without Lassie being discovered.

Our flight to Kathmandu was the following day so we spent a night in Biratnagar in a Dak Bungalow, a government-run guesthouse for travelers. The metal-framed beds with hemp straps for the base were ridden with bedbugs. The bedbugs probably lived between the straps. Ugh! We couldn't wait to get of there. Later that morning we hired a couple of rickshaws, which took the four of us, and Lassie, to the airport. We had to wait around for several hours before finally boarding a DC-3 bound for Kathmandu. In those days, everyone knew everyone else in Kathmandu. My mother knew all the pilots since they were frequent customers in her bar and restaurant. Two pilots were going to be on duty the day our plane was coming in from Biratnagar. She asked them to watch out for us in Biratnagar and help us get on board. Little did they know they had to give permission to have a little dog brought on to the plane as well!

9

Altar Boys

I was eleven when I started class seven. We called them class instead of grade. I made friends with a girl who sat in front of me in study hall. Rani was three or four years older and a lot more mature than I was. She was a boarder and, like me, her family lived in the area, just outside Darjeeling. She seemed to know a lot about "the facts of life" and appeared willing to enlighten me. Having grown up in a convent from the age of four, I had no clue of how babies were born, for instance. I never really thought about it. One day, when Rani and I were talking about our families, she told me that she had seven siblings and that one of her sisters was expecting a child.

"That is so exciting," I said. "God must have answered her prayers."

"What are you talking about?"

"Isn't that how you get babies?"

"By praying to God?" she replied in disbelief. "No, that's not how you get babies!"

"Well, how does one have a baby if not by praying to God? That's what the nuns tell us. Some girl told me that when a boy kisses a girl, she could get pregnant. Maybe that's why the nuns don't want us to see the kissing scenes in the movies. They don't want us to get any ideas."

"Gosh, you are so stupid. No, you don't get pregnant if a boy kisses you. Hasn't anyone told you how a girl really gets pregnant?"

"No. I never really thought too much about it."

"A girl can become pregnant when she has sex with a boy."

"Oh, what's that? What is sex?"

Rani looked at me, and it suddenly dawned on her how naïve I was. She became embarrassed and didn't want to take it any further. All she said was, "Well, you're too young for me to explain. You will learn about it soon enough. At least you know now that you don't get babies by praying and you can't get babies from kissing."

I wanted her to tell me more but she refused to go on and changed the subject.

"Can you keep a secret?" she suddenly asked.

"Of course!" I replied, getting quite excited. "Are you pregnant?"

"No, of course not! There's this altar boy that I really like and he likes me too. I met him over winter holidays but my older brothers won't allow me to see him. He wants to write to me but I can't let him mail me letters because you know how the nuns are. If they censor my letters, I could get into big trouble if they let my brothers know. Do you think you can help me?"

"Of course, what do you want me to do?"

"The altar boy's name is Reginald, the good-looking one

who usually helps the priest out every other Sunday. He looks for me in church and every time our eyes meet, I get so excited my heart beats very fast."

"Oh, I remember seeing the handsome boy. He usually works with another good-looking boy who has dark skin."

"Yeah, that's him. Reginald is Nepali and his friend is from Bihar."

"What's his friend's name?"

"I don't know. I've never talked with him."

"So, what do you want me to do?" By this time, I had become totally fascinated.

"Reginald and I had planned to write to each other. He thought it would be safer if we had 'go-betweens' and this is where you can help. Reginald's friend will deliver his letter to you and you will take mine to him. I've thought a lot about it: I think that the best time for the two of you to meet is after break, just before study hall. It always takes a while for the girls to get back into study hall. During this time you can run down past the senior play field and meet him near the south gate where he will enter the schoolyard without being detected. You will exchange the letters and get back to study hall in time. I know you're a fast runner."

"This means he has to sneak onto the school grounds. You know he will get into deep trouble if he gets caught."

"They both promised me that they would be very careful and would not take any risks."

"Okay. How will he know what I look like?"

"I told Reginald that the next time I see him in church I will give him a special signal and he will know it's the girl sitting next to me who will deliver my letters."

"Gosh, you two have really got everything figured out."

"Yeah, we've been planning this for some time now and we were just waiting for the right time to start. It looks like you're the one who can make it happen."

I was flattered by the compliment and excited to be involved in a romantic intrigue.

"So, when should we start?"

"I have to give him the signal in church to let him know when I'm ready, so I will let him know this Sunday when he comes to mass."

"What's your signal?"

"He and I worked that out: if I touch my head when he looks at me it means I am ready to receive his letters. I will then touch your arm and he will know that you will be our letter carrier."

"How will I know when he has a letter for you?"

"He will give me a different sign when he has a letter for me."

"What sort of sign?"

"He told me to look for him on the hillside opposite the study hall. He's off from school on Tuesday evenings so if he has a letter for me he will be on the hillside behind the trees and he will light up a cigarette. So we have to look for his cigarette."

This was all very exciting. I couldn't wait for things to start happening. That Sunday, I sat next to Rani in church and we waited for Reginald to come out with the priest. We were disappointed when another altar boy was there instead. Two or three Sundays went by and there was no sign of him. Finally, when we had all but given up hope, he appeared. I was just as nervous as Rani. I observed both of them closely. When their eyes met, she reached for her head and I saw him make a slight nod. It was on.

The following Tuesday I was at study hall seated behind Rani as usual, doing my homework. She turned and whispered, "Look at the hillside, do you see anyone?"

I had forgotten it was Tuesday. I looked across the senior field onto the hillside outside the school boundary and scanned the bushes. Nothing. It was already dusk and hard to make out much, and then I saw a tiny red glow. I realized it was the glow coming from the end of a cigarette. It was enough to focus on that area. I finally saw Reginald and his friend.

"I see the tiny glow. If you focus around there for a while, you will see both of them," I whispered.

"Oh yes, I see them."

"So, now what?"

"I'll tell you later after study hall."

Later that evening, as we dressed for bed, Rani told me the details. I was to meet Reginald's friend on Thursday at the designated area and make the exchange. When Thursday arrived, I did what I was supposed to do and went to meet my counterpart. He introduced himself as David and seemed like a nice and agreeable boy. For the next several months, David and I became couriers for our lovesick friends. After several encounters with David, he asked me if it was okay for him to write to me. I liked him and so we agreed that we would write to each other as well. It was the first time I was awakened to fluttery feelings inside.

The exchanges continued without mishap and everyone seemed happy. Before the end of the year, however, I had to break the news to Rani that I would be not becoming back as a boarder the following year. She knew what a rough year I had been having with Mother Dolores.

"I'm really sorry I will not be able to continue being your letter courier. I had fun doing it. David and I have become good friends too."

She looked sad but I realized it was more than just that. "What is it?"

"I won't be coming back to school next year."

"What! Why? Are you changing schools? Did your brothers find out about the letters?"

"No, they don't know about the letters. I know this will come as a shock, but my brothers want me home now that both my parents have passed away. I think they want me to help out with the chores. They also told me it was time for me to get married."

"I can't believe what you're telling me. You haven't finished school and you're so young. They can't be serious."

Rani was going to turn fifteen. It turned out that she was almost four years older than me and had started school later than the rest of us. Her mother had kept her home to help out with chores and only later, at her father's insistence, was she finally allowed to attend school.

"Please don't tell anyone since I haven't mentioned to anyone yet that I'm not coming back."

I didn't know what to say. I was sad to think I wasn't going to see her any more. It wasn't fair. How could her brothers make her marry at such a young age? I had learned a lot from her that year and we had become very close. I also had grown up quite a bit. We promised each other that we would stay in touch. We never saw each other again, however, especially after school closed abruptly the following year due to the border war. I have often wondered what became of her.

10

Becoming a Day Scholar

Apart from isolated incidents—like running away from school, befriending Rani, and being terrorized by Mother Dolores—most of the years I spent at Loreto are a blur, one year merging into the next. My courier job for Rani and Reginald helped me keep my sense of humour and was a diversion from Mother Dolores' harassments. I was becoming restless and desperately wanted to become a day scholar so that I could live at home. There were two main reasons: first, both my mother and my sister were no longer home and I missed them desperately. I also felt I could help Popo look after Bobby since he probably missed them as well. Secondly, I was becoming increasingly afraid of Mother Dolores.

Mother Dolores taught the elocution classes and had taken over the school kitchen when the previous nun in charge was assigned to a different school. I must admit the food improved immensely when Mother Dolores took charge—especially the scrambled eggs, which were no longer hard and likely to bounce off your plate. Loreto nuns wore long black habits with veils that covered their heads and went down to their shoulders. Their hands and faces were the only parts of their bodies that were exposed. Mother Dolores was a portly woman with a round red face. When she lost her temper, her face went beet-red. There may have been girls who liked her, but she was my nemesis and she disliked me intensely. I wondered if it was simply because I wasn't English or because I had the nerve to challenge her in class one day. After that, she took any opportunity to disparage me in front of the class or the whole school.

What happened was that Mother Dolores was going to be directing a Gilbert and Sullivan play. Her announcement came during elocution class.

"You probably already know, girls, that we are putting on *H.M.S. Pinafore* this year. I'm happy to tell you that I will be directing it and I'm expecting everyone in all my elocution classes to take part." She continued, "You Chinese girls, can be excused from the play and you can sit at the back of the classroom while we practice." I was sure she was mainly addressing the two Chinese girls who were recently admitted to the school. The sisters were just beginning to learn English and it seemed reasonable that they would be excused. However, because of the way she made the announcement, it sounded very insensitive; it upset me. There were only a handful of Chinese girls in the entire school and, for the first time, I was made aware that I was different from the others. I was neither Anglo nor was I Indian. That night before I went to bed, I looked at myself in the mirror and found that I was indeed Chinese. I decided that I would join the two girls and sit at the back of the classroom.

For several practice sessions I sat happily at the back of the classroom with the other two Chinese girls reading, doing homework, working on a needlework project, or quietly chatting. When Mother Dolores saw me sitting back there, she stopped the class recital mid-song, pointed to me, and shouted.

"You! What are you doing back there? I didn't give you permission to sit back there!" I don't think she ever called me by my name.

I looked up in shock and replied, "You said Chinese girls didn't have to participate in the play."

Looking at me and getting red in the face, she said, "I did not give you permission to sit back there!"

"You said Chinese girls don't have to participate, and I'm Chinese."

"How dare you talk back to me! Come up here at once!"

I went up to the front of the class, petrified and upset. She called me a liar and continued to verbally abuse me in front of the entire class. I continued to protest and some of the other girls came to my defence but she ignored us all. She had lost all composure. She began saying things about my family that weren't true.

"You should ask your father to take you back to Kalimpong."

"We don't come from Kalimpong, why should he take me back there?" I asked.

"Don't you dare talk back to me!" She shouted and continued with other bizarre statements until I finally broke down and cried uncontrollably. She started laughing and pointed her finger at me with her red face getting ever redder.

"Look at her, just look at her, she's become hysterical! Go at once and put your head under the tap and don't come back until you stop that."

I ran out of the classroom and stayed in the bathroom until the bell rang. After that incident, Mother Dolores found other ways to harass me, and I began to fear the sight of her. I decided that the only way I could avoid her was to become a day scholar.

Finally, Papa came to visit. I was so happy to see him. I told him I was very unhappy in school and wanted to be a day scholar the following year. I said I missed Mummy and Pu-Chin very much. My father had started winding down Park Restaurant, and recently Mummy had sent for Borjee and Ayah to join her in Nepal. I knew I would miss Borjee a lot when I went home, but I felt even sorrier for Bobby who was so attached to Ayah. I told Papa I wanted to be home to help Popo look after Bobby. To my surprise, he agreed with me, but he told me I had to write to Mummy and get her permission.

It wasn't easy to change one's status from a boarder to a day scholar. First, you had to get parental consent. Parents had to write to Mother Superior to inform her that they had given their permission for their child's status to be changed. When Mother Superior got this, she gave the boarder her approval to become a day scholar. I was nervous about writing to my mother. We all suspected that the nuns censored our letters, and I had confirmed this through personal experience. I didn't want them to find out what I had in mind.

One day I was summoned by Mother John Bergman. Agnes, the parlour maid, came to look for me and told me that I would find her in the Assembly Hall. When I arrived, I found her waiting for me. She greeted me kindly and asked how I was and how everything was at home. I was puzzled by her concern, which came out of the blue. I answered that everything was well at home as far as I was concerned. Then I noticed that she was holding an aerogram letter from overseas, and guessed it was from my sister. I became excited. She handed me the letter and it was indeed from Pu-Chin. Before Mother John Bergman dismissed me, she touched my shoulder and said, "We will pray for your parents." Thanking her, I took the letter and found a quiet place outside to read it. I noticed that it had been opened. This annoyed me very much. In my sister's letter, she expressed that she was concerned about the relationship between our parents, and wondered if I had noticed any changes. I was shocked. I had no idea that there was anything amiss. It hadn't even entered my mind that things could be wrong at home. I became worried but was more upset that my letter had been opened and read.

If Mother Dolores found out about my intention to become a day scholar, I was afraid she would use it to humiliate me further. I had to get permission from my mother and I had no choice but to write to her. I decided to write my entire letter backwards. I used to read many of Enid Blyton's books and particularly loved "The Famous Five" adventure series. (Enid Blyton was to us as J. K. Rowling is to young readers of today.) "The Famous Five" series was about the adventures of a group of four kids: three siblings, their cousin Georgina, and also her dog. Georgina was the brains behind their wild adventures, and constantly got the group into and out of trouble. She was a tomboy and hated wearing dresses, so she wore pants most of the time, an unusual thing for girls to do at that time. She also wore her hair very short and told everyone her name was George so that people would assume she was a boy. She felt that she could get away with a lot more pretending to be a boy. I felt the same.

I got the idea of writing my letters backwards from one of their adventures. When I finished writing my letter, I was pleased with my efforts. Looking it over, however, I realized my mother wouldn't be able to read it. So I carefully wrote in tiny print at the bottom of the letter, **"Mummy, if you want to read this, you must hold it in front of the mirror!"** Fortunately, the nuns didn't question me about this, and I was eventually given permission. The following year, in March 1962, I returned to Loreto as a day scholar.

11

Wish Realized

It was a whole new adjustment. I had slept in Popo's room over holiday weekends, but now I had to live in her room permanently, with Bobby. I began to learn Popo's idiosyncrasies. I learned that fresh milk was delivered to our flat every morning and Popo made it her duty to boil it in her bedroom. It was a peculiar habit of hers, to boil the milk in her bedroom rather than in the kitchen. She used a single electric burner that she kept at the hearth solely for this purpose. As far as I can remember, she never used the fireplace in her bedroom. One morning, she woke up, went to fetch the milk, brought it back to her room, and put it on to boil. She was in a particularly good mood and wanted to tell us Chinese stories while we were getting dressed for school. We loved her stories even though we had heard them many times. We asked her to repeat our favorite one. The three of us, Popo, Bobby and I, were in a happy mood and forgot the milk was on the stove. It boiled over! Our happy mood spoiled in an instant. Popo was so furious and blamed me for not watching over the milk. I don't know why she got so angry with me but it made me mad; I told her it was unfair for her to blame me. She continued to grumble until we ran off to school. I fumed all day and decided that when I got home that evening, I would move into Pu-Chin's unused bedroom. It was turned into a study after she left home but was infrequently used. I had been hoping to find a way to move in there, and now I had the opportunity.

When I returned from school, I immediately went to Papa and asked him if I could move into Pu-Chin's old room. I told him I was old enough to have my own room and besides, the studio wasn't used much any more. He seemed to prefer to write his memoir at the desk in his bedroom rather than in the study. He agreed readily, and I was so ecstatic I immediately started moving my things in. When Popo saw me moving into the studio she got upset and started crying.

"I brought you up and cared for you ever since you were born. You are moving out of my room just because I blamed you for letting the milk boil over. You are very ungrateful. I'm sorry I yelled at you and I'm sorry I hurt your feelings." She apologized over and over. I was beginning to feel badly but didn't want to give in.

"Popo, of course I know that you brought us up. I still love you. I was angry with you this morning, but I'm not angry any more, and I'm not moving out because you yelled at me. I want to move into Gigi's room because no one is using it right now and it will give you and Bobby more space. It will be good for me too because I'll be able to study better. I'm not going far away; I'm only going down the hall." I gave her all the reasons I could think of. Even though I was sorry to have hurt her feelings, I held firm and tried to convince her it was best for everyone. She saw I wasn't going to change my mind. Inwardly, I was on cloud nine.

Being a day scholar was very different. I had to get up early, rush to get dressed, eat breakfast with the family, and then dash off to school. Sometimes I would get a craving for a Chinese breakfast, something we never had in boarding school, and ask Papa if it was all right to run down to Chef Ong's teahouse. He was always agreeable, and Bobby and I would run down to pick it up. Chinese breakfast usually consisted of rice porridge, long fried bread, and green onion pies, along with an assortment of pickles. The long fried bread was like a savoury donut: deep-fried, light, and airy. The green onion pies were flaky pies three inches around and about an inch thick made of flour, water, pork fat, green onions, and sprinkled with sesame seeds. They were mouth-wateringly delicious! Chef Ong's green onion pies were the best in the world. It took us twenty minutes to run down to the teahouse and back: downhill to the teahouse, uphill home. We didn't mind because we loved having the special food when we got back. Popo always started cooking the rice porridge, or congee, early in the morning, and it was still cooking when we returned with the savouries. After breakfast I would rush off to school; it took me twenty to twenty-five minutes to get there.

12

Bengali Class

At the start of the new school year we were being assigned to our classes. A close friend of mine had been taking French. "You should try and get into French class. You'll love it." Anna said. "It's more fun than Bengali." When I went to the nun in charge of the language department and asked permission to take French, she looked at me and responded:

"Darling, why do you want to take French?"

"I'd like to take French because Anna is taking French and she loves it."

The nun continued looking at me intently and said, "But there's no reason for you to take French. There's no possibility that you would ever go to France. It would be a waste of your time and a waste of your parents' money. I think it would be more useful for you to take either Hindi or Bengali. I suggest the best thing for you would be to take Hindi. I'm sorry I cannot give you permission to take French."

I was shattered when I heard what she told me. "But," I

retorted, "Anna is taking French and I don't see why I can't take it as well."

"Well, Anna's different. She comes from a privileged family and will surely travel to France some day."

It didn't seem fair. I walked away, disappointed. I enrolled in Bengali instead of Hindi.

Bengali class was held in the southwest corner of the roller-skating rink that served as a multi-purpose hall for different events, such as the end-of-year costume parade and senior dances. Most importantly, this was where we had recess when it rained, and during the monsoon, it rained and it rained. The rink was a large room situated directly below the classrooms, about fifty feet wide by two hundred feet long, with beautiful wooden floors. There were windows on both sides. On the east side, the windows faced the senior playground and netball court (girls didn't play basketball in those days) and on the west side, they overlooked the lower division playground. It was the most pivotal place in school. All important things happened there: friendships were made or broken, the latest gossip was heard, secrets and stories were exchanged.

It wasn't until August or September that I noticed a change in the mood of the school. About this time my best friend Susan, her brother, and their Chinese mother suddenly left town for good. They lived in the same apartment building but on the floor below us. When I became a day scholar, Susan and I walked to and from school together every day, and we became best friends. Like me, she loved horseback riding. Whenever we got permission and pocket money from our parents, we would go riding. Sometimes her brother and Bobby would accompany us but we preferred riding by ourselves, because her older brother galloped too fast, and Bobby, being so much younger, was too slow. If we didn't ride, we just hung around the stables. My father invited Susan's family to dinner quite frequently. She and her brother spent winter breaks with their father in Thailand. She told me that her father, who was English, alternated between living in Thailand and England. I didn't know much about her family other than that her mother was originally from Peking. As children, we were taught never to ask personal questions of anyone, particularly of adults. I'm not sure whether it was something we learned in school or whether it was a Chinese custom. Consequently, we never asked questions in those days.

Their departure happened fast, with only a brief explanation that they were going to England to join their father. On the day of their departure, my family and I walked them to the taxi stand. We said goodbye and watched them get into the car. Then, they were gone. I was devastated. We never saw them again. After that, my father, as well as other friends of his, seemed more anxious than normal. I didn't know why, but there was a sense of foreboding. A few weeks later, in early October, something happened in Bengali class that changed life forever.

13

Conflict

On an early October morning in 1962, Miss Banerjee, our Bengali instructor, was trying to calm a classroom full of hysterical girls. We had just learned that India and China were on the brink of war over a border dispute. There were rumours that the Indian government might close the borders, which would have serious implications for the school since many girls came from neighbouring countries. If the borders closed, these girls would not be able to return home for winter holidays. I still remember Miss Banerjee's voice when she tried to talk to us above the nervous chatter.

"I just can't believe you girls," she said. "Here you are worried about whether the Indian government is going to close the borders when you should be worried about whether there might be a Third World War!"

Most of us had no clue what she was saying. We were in one of the remotest parts of the world, secluded in the Himalayan Mountains. How could we know what was going on beyond our small world of Darjeeling?

"Miss Banerjee," someone asked, "what do you mean? What are you talking about? What 'Third World War'?"

"You girls are so ignorant; don't you read the newspapers or listen to the radio?" She sounded exasperated. We were only twelve- and thirteen-year olds. Who had radios in boarding school, let alone newspapers? She must have been really upset to forget that most of us did not have access to such things.

"Miss Banerjee, please tell us what's happening! What are you talking about? We want to know what's going on."

She finally realized how truly uninformed we were about what went on beyond the walls of Loreto Convent. She tried to explain in terms that we could understand.

"The United States and the Soviet Union are on the brink of war, a nuclear war," she emphasized. "The United States has discovered a secret Soviet missile base on the island of Cuba, very close to their country. Now they have found out that the Soviets are intending to increase the number of missiles aimed at American cities. The U.S. sees this as a threat and has imposed a naval blockade."

"Miss Banerjee, what's a naval blockade?" someone asked.

"A naval blockade means that any ship entering this zone will be searched by the U.S. Navy. If the ship is carrying weapons it will be turned back. The Soviets are outraged by this act and have refused to go along. The tension between the two countries has reached a climax. As we are speaking, they are at a standoff, and things don't look good. If they go to war, the whole world will be affected."

We all became very quiet as her words sank in; for just a little while, our own problems diminished. A few days later, Mother Superior announced at the school assembly that Loreto was going to close early so the girls from neighbouring countries could return home in case the borders closed. To our delight there would be no final exams and most of us would be promoted to the next class. When the time arrived, we said our goodbyes amidst tears and joy: tears, because we didn't know what the future would bring or how soon we might see each other again, and joy, because school was closing and everyone was going home.

I was thrilled that school had ended early and looked forward to a long lazy winter vacation in which I could read all my favourite books and eat Popo's yummy home-cooked food. I planned on taking frequent horseback rides and wondered how I would talk Popo into giving me two rupees everyday for that purpose. Given the chance, I would have spent all my time and allowance at the stables. I also started to plan long hikes with Bobby and close friends, like the ones that Gigi took me on before she went away. I wanted to explore the whole town and looked forward to playing games in the street with the neighbourhood kids. There were no cars in our part of town so our parents didn't have to worry about us. Things were totally safe. Finally, I wanted to spend more time with my father. It was going to be a wonderful extended holiday.

14

Pancakes to Prison

School had been closed for less than two weeks when the war broke out along the border between India and China. It was the twentieth of October 1962. Papa had been glued to his favourite Zenith radio for days, and he told us what was happening. He was disturbed at the way the Indian government mishandled troop mobilization and felt bad for the Indian soldiers who suffered high casualties.

"I can't imagine," he said, shaking his head in frustration as he was explaining to me, "why the Indian government is so hopeless. They have sent the soldiers to fight the Chinese in the high mountains in just their regular cotton clothing. It is already mid-October. Many are just freezing to death. They didn't even get a chance to fight. And, at the same time, the soldiers have been issued guns without enough ammunition. Can you imagine that? I have fought in a war and I know what I'm talking about. How can they treat their own soldiers like that? Hopeless, just hopeless!"

"Papa, I don't understand why India and China are fighting," I said to him. "I thought they were supposed to be brothers."

"I know. Things change. The two countries are fighting over the border areas in the Ladakh desert, which is in the northwestern corner of India, near Pakistan. China has always considered this area part of Tibet. In fact, the people in that area are ethnically Tibetan, not Indian. When the British ruled India they drew up a boundary line and claimed this area as part of India. They wanted it to be a buffer between India and China. They were also worried about both Chinese and Russian expansion into India." He continued, "The two countries are also fighting on the eastern border, north of the Assam area. This is closer to us. It was the British again who decided to claim this territory as part of India. They pushed the boundary from the foothills of Assam all the way up to the Crest of the Himalayas. China is very upset because they have always believed this area belonged to Tibet and, of course, the Chinese believe that Tibet is part of China."

I watched Papa as he tried to describe the situation to me, becoming more and more upset. His handsome face hardened and his eyes became very intense. I didn't quite understand what he was trying to relate to me and I wanted to change the subject. I was sorry to hear about the soldiers freezing to death, but the war seemed far away, and irrelevant to our quiet lives in our remote little town. Out of frustration and sympathy for the soldiers fighting at the border, Papa did some fundraising among the Chinese community and sent money to support the Indian army. He really disliked the Chinese Communist regime.

* * *

On the last Friday in October, my father and I were in the kitchen getting ready for four o'clock tea. I had missed this ritual since I was in school most of the year but during winter holidays I looked forward to four o'clock tea every day. Living in India in those days, most of us continued to follow the British ritual, although our family usually had an assortment of Chinese snacks rather than biscuits, cakes, and cucumber sandwiches. Our snacks were usually savoury or spicy and, from time to time, I asked Papa to pick up singaras (Bengali samosas) from the local teashop. I loved them! On this particular day, my father was teaching me how to make Chinese pancakes—a specialty of Anhui Province, where he and my mother lived during the Sino-Japanese War, and where my sister was born. These pancakes were different from Chef Ong's flaky onion pies. They were thin and flat, more like a French crepe.

"I think you know how to make them now, so finish the rest by yourself," Papa said as he joined Popo and Bobby at the table. When I finished making the pancakes, I joined them, rather pleased that I was able to make my favourite dish all by myself. We were all happy and looking forward to our afternoon family get-together when there was a knock on the front door. My father asked me to go see who it was. I opened the door to a stranger standing there. He was a middle-aged Tibetan man dressed in regular western clothes instead of Tibetan dress. He wanted to speak to my father. I told him that we had just sat down to tea and asked him to come back later. He said it was very important that he see him right away. I didn't like his rude manner and reluctantly went to fetch my father.

My father spoke with the stranger for quite a while then returned to the table with an annoyed look.

"Who is that man, Papa? What does he want?" I asked him.

"I don't know him. I thought I knew all the Tibetans in town." Then he continued in a serious tone, "You all continue with your tea, I have to go down to the police station to answer a few questions but I'll be back soon." Looking directly at me he said, "Yin-Chin, darling, in the meantime, take care of everything." Then he was gone. We all sat in silence, staring at each other with a strange uneasy feeling. Finally Popo said, "Let's continue with our tea, Papa will be back soon." Later that evening, Papa did not return. He did not return the next day, or the next.

Several days went by and still there was no sign or word from him. We became very anxious. I had just turned thirteen the month before. My brother was eight, and my grandmother was—well, I really didn't know—she was just Popo, and old, and she didn't speak Hindi or English, only Chinese.

The days went by, and we became even more frightened and didn't know what to do. Then, a Chinese man appeared at the front door. He introduced himself as Mr. Lee. I was surprised to see him. Although we were Chinese, our friends were mostly Tibetan, Nepali, or Indian. I knew only two Chinese girls, the pair who were in my elocution class.

I looked at Mr. Lee who seemed kind and in no way threatening. We invited him in. I could tell he was a Hakka, in his mid-thirties, and nice-looking. He was sympathetic and sincere although he didn't tell us much about himself or his family. For some reason, I didn't ask him questions either. He obviously wanted to deliver us a message and seemed concerned about our well-being. He began to explain why he had unexpectedly appeared.

"I'm a shoemaker and I own a shop down at the bazaar," he said. "I have been appointed by members in the Chinese community to come and help your family. I don't know if you know, but your parents have always been supportive of the Chinese community ever since they arrived in Darjeeling. We heard that your father was arrested and felt it was time for us to repay his generosity. The community appointed me to come and help you and that's why I'm here."

"My father, arrested? What do you mean?" I continued, "A man came around tea time a few days ago and asked to speak to Papa. Then he left with the man telling us that the police just wanted to ask him a few questions down at the police station and he never came back. Why did they arrest him? Where is he?"

"I'm afraid I don't know where he is but I will try to find out tomorrow. As soon as I find out anything I will be back. Did your father know this man?"

"No, he was Tibetan but Papa didn't know him. He was surprised too since he thought he knew all the Tibetans in town."

Over the course of the next several days, Mr. Lee found out that my father had been locked up in the Darjeeling jail without being charged. He was under suspicion of being a spy for the Peoples Republic of China.

"That is ridiculous," I said to Mr. Lee when he returned. "Everyone knows Papa hates the Communist Chinese, why would he be a spy for China? It doesn't make sense."

"Apparently," Mr. Lee answered, "the officials have somehow found out that your mother is in Nepal and they are using this as an excuse to build a case against your father."

"Why?" I questioned him.

"Well, as you know, the government of Nepal has friendly ties with China whereas India has broken off its diplomatic relations with China."

"Mr. Lee, that still doesn't make sense at all," I repeated.

"I know it doesn't. Many things don't make sense lately. I will try to get your father out on bail. The Chinese community has offered to raise money to pay his bail. Meanwhile, you should go around to your parents' friends and ask them to help you. I also heard the food in jail is very bad so I would like to suggest that you ask your Popo to prepare food for your father every day. I'm sure he would be grateful."

Every day for the following month, Popo prepared special meals and Sailee would walk with Bobby and me down to the jail every afternoon to deliver his dinner to him. Lassie, of course, always accompanied us since he followed us everywhere. Sailee was Bobby's new nanny. After Ayah left to join my mother in Nepal, my father hired a Darjeeling woman of Nepalese ethnicity. It took Bobby some time to accept Sailee since he had known Ayah all his life and missed her enormously.

We never saw our father in those weeks and had no idea whether he actually got the food we brought. When we arrived at the jail, the prison guard would come out and make me taste the food before he carried it in. It irritated me that I was made to taste it since I had been doing this every day for several weeks. One day I simply lost my temper when the jailor told me to taste the food.

"Why are you asking me to do this every single time? You know who we are. We've brought this food for our father. Why do you think we would want to poison our own father?"

When she heard my outburst, Sailee became concerned. "Come, baby, let's go home. He knows you don't want to poison your father. It's just his duty." She quickly dragged me away. The next day, when we arrived at the jail to drop off Papa's food, the prison guard was nicer. He asked us how we were and then said he had a message from my father. "Your father wants you to bring that flat Tibetan bread and momo as often as you can."

"Really? I didn't know he liked tsampa that much. Okay, we'll do our best."

I never liked tsampa. To me, it tasted like cardboard. It is dry flat bread made from roasted barley flour about seven inches round and a quarter inch thick. I concluded that being in jail must have brought back memories of my father's childhood days growing up in Kangding. I told Popo about Papa's request so she gave us money every two or three days so that we could buy tsampa at a Tibetan café on the way to jail. Other times we went to a different café to pick up Tibetan momo to give Papa some variety. (Momo is equivalent to Chinese boiled dumplings, just bigger and coarser.)

Years later, Papa told me that he used to share his food with some of the other inmates who rarely received food from home. They had never eaten Chinese or Tibetan food before and loved to share his meals. He was always happy to provide them a little pleasure in the otherwise sad life they had in jail.

It took us forty-five minutes to walk to the jail—located about two to three hundred feet below the bazaar—and close to an hour to return due to the trek being all uphill. We followed the same routine every day, and each day we had to pass a large concrete windowless building: the

Darjeeling Jail: Although the photo was taken in 2001, not much had changed since 1962.

slaughterhouse. The stench was terrible. We had to hold our breaths and cover our noses and mouths as we passed. On occasion we would see a single cow being dragged into the building against its will.

We dreaded passing this place and listening to the mournful cries of the animals that seemed to know they were not long for this world. They, too, were locked up against their will, and had no control over their destiny.

15

Seeking Help

A few days after his first visit, Mr. Lee returned to our house to tell us that he wanted to take me to the Chinese temple down at the bazaar. I was mystified; I had never been to a Chinese temple. On the other hand, I was, of course, familiar with the Roman Catholic Church, having been brought up in Loreto. I had visited Hindu and Buddhist temples in Kathmandu, and was also familiar with the Kali Temple in Calcutta where Ayah had taken us during winter holidays. She was a Kali devotee and felt she needed to go to the temple whenever she was in town. Bobby and I were always terrified to visit the Kali Temple, a dark, dank, and crowded place. Its walls were smeared with blood from sacrificed animals. The mixture of sweat, humidity, animal blood, and incense created an odour that made us queasy. We had to be well-behaved and stuck to Ayah like glue since we did not want to get lost in there, or worse, be destroyed by Kali.

I had no idea what to expect. When we entered, it was like nothing I had ever experienced. It was serene and clean and Mr. Lee and I were the only ones there. There were several religious icons on pedestals around the room in varied sizes, but I had no idea who they depicted and what they represented. Like the Kali Temple and the Catholic Church, there was the ubiquitous smell of incense.

The keeper of the temple came out and I was introduced to a young woman in her twenties dressed in a simple flowing robe. After Mr. Lee spoke to her for a few minutes she gestured to me to follow her into an inner chamber. She told me to sit on the floor while she went to fetch a cylindrical box. In it were dozens of thin long wooden sticks, each with writing on it. She handed me the box and told me to shake it, dump the sticks onto the floor, and then pick out six. I did as I was told without any clue what it all meant. She looked at the sticks I had picked out, and by the expression on her face, it didn't bode well. Later, Mr. Lee explained that she was reading my fortune and the fortune of my father. The results, apparently, were inconclusive and Mr. Lee suggested that we return after a few days later and try our luck again. It was all quite strange. My parents had never talked about Chinese religion. I think they must have felt that I had enough religion in the convent. The only thing I do remember in connection with Chinese religion is what Popo would say when we didn't finish the food in our bowls. "*Pu Sa sen chi le!*" (Buddha will be angry!) I didn't know who Pu Sa was but I always ate up everything on my plate.

Several days after the visit to the Chinese temple, Mr. Lee returned to tell us that he was sorry. "I failed in getting your father out on bail. I tried very hard to convince the authorities that he was a good and hardworking citizen, and has always been anti-Communist, that he was not a spy. I did not succeed." Maybe this was the bad news the fortune-teller had seen. "However," he continued, "I have some good news. I may be able to get permission for you to visit your Papa. I will let you know in a day or two. By the way, I should tell you that you are being watched and you need to be alert. Just to be on the safe side, you should always keep your curtains closed." Then he looked at Bobby and me with great seriousness and continued, "You two should never go out alone under any circumstances."

Mr. Lee's statement was odd. Not go out alone? We had never been restricted before. Darjeeling was such a safe place for children.

"Why can't we go out alone? Why are we being watched?" Bobby asked. "Is it because Papa is in jail? We've always gone out alone. What will happen if we go out alone? Is somebody going to hurt us? I want to play with my friends in the street." Bobby was a happy, good-natured little boy and had many friends in the neighbourhood. They always hung around together and played in the street. He came home only when dinner was ready. It was hard for him to understand why all of a sudden it was unsafe to go out.

Mr. Lee looked at the unhappy boy, "I know you want to go out and play, but lately things have changed, Bobby. Many Chinese have disappeared during the night and no one knows what happened to them. Maybe nothing will happen to you, but we can't afford to take any chances. Local people are looking at us Chinese differently now. Promise me that you will be careful and listen to what I'm saying."

"Okay, we promise," we replied. However, we were not happy about it, and I still did not fully understand the impact of his words.

"Now, what I suggest you do right away," Mr. Lee continued, "is go through your parents' documents and see if you find any letters. Get rid of them because they might get you in trouble, especially ones your mother has sent from Nepal."

"Why? Do you think someone will come and search our house? What are they looking for?"

"It's possible someone from the C.I.D. will come to look for things to harm your father."

"C.I.D.?"

"Central Intelligence Department."

"But I can't read Chinese," I said, "How can I tell which papers are harmful?"

"Well, then perhaps you should burn everything that looks like letters. After you burn them, flush them down the toilet. Don't throw them in the rubbish bin because that's the first place the C.I.D. people will look."

"What if we find documents that look really important?" I asked him. "Should we burn those too?"

"Well, if you find documents that you think are really important, hide them away in a very safe place." All of a sudden, I felt we were in the middle of an exciting adventure.

After Mr. Lee's instructions, we told Popo that we were going to visit some very close friends of our parents. They were Tibetan. Maybe they could help us get Papa out on bail, I said. Popo was pleased with this idea, so Bobby and I went out together. I remembered when our parents used to take us to visit these people. I never liked going to their house because they had many little dogs that barked furiously whenever anyone came to the door and seemed to particularly dislike children. When we reached their house and knocked on the door, the dogs started barking like crazy just as we expected. Then Uncle finally came to the door. (Following the Indian or Chinese tradition, we called all our parents' friends either uncle or aunty.) He was surprised to see us.

"Hello, Uncle. We came to ask you for your help. I don't know if you know, they put Papa in jail and we haven't seen him for days. We have no one to turn to. Can you help us get him out on bail?"

"Yes, I heard about your Papa," he said, "and I'm truly sorry about what happened, but there is nothing we can do to help you." Before we could make any further pleas he quickly shut the door in our faces. We were dumbfounded because we considered him to be one of my father's closest friends.

Not knowing what else to do, I decided to go and see Mother Superior at Loreto Convent. I was sure that she would help us. We had always been told time and again that the nuns were there to help those in need. I don't know what they could have done for us but I thought maybe they could at least tell the court that they had known my parents for many years and that we were good people. Park Restaurant had often catered the school's annual picnic and other events throughout the years and always made donations to the school. I felt confident that I would find help there.

Once again I took Bobby with me. We became especially close during those days, mindful of Mr. Lee's warning never to venture out alone. When we arrived at the convent, we went directly into the parlour and rang the bell. Minutes after, we were warmly greeted by Agnes. Besides her many duties, her main one was to greet visitors in the parlour. She would then locate the persons the visitors had come to see. We all liked Agnes who was a gentle and kind person. As far as I can remember, she had always worked at Loreto. Boarders were always excited to see her come into the dining room or study hall, each girl hoping she had a visitor.

"Hello, Yin-Chin, it's so nice to see you again. All the girls have gone home now and it is so quiet and lonely these days. How is your family? What can I do for you?"

I explained to her all that had happened. "Things have turned upside down at home and I thought Mother Superior could help us. Can we see her?"

Agnes then went to look for Mother Superior and after several minutes, returned with her. We greeted each other politely and I introduced Bobby, and explained all over again what had happened to our family over the past few weeks. She looked very concerned.

"Mother Superior, I was hoping you could do something to get our father released from jail. We don't know why he was put there. As you know, our mother is not in the country and Pu-Chin is studying in America; it's only the two of us at home with our grandmother. I've been asking friends of the family but none have been able to offer help. We have no one else to turn to. You've known our parents for many years."

She looked at us sympathetically, "Yes, we know your parents and they are lovely people. They have been good to the convent over the years, but I'm so sorry, my darlings, at this time, we cannot help you. It must be due to what's happening between China and India and we just simply don't get involved in politics. We will, however, say special prayers for your father and for your whole family." As she escorted us to the front door she said, "Please convey my regards to your dear grandmother."

That was the end of it. Two letdowns in one day. By the time we returned home, I knew that we were truly on our own except for the mysterious Mr. Lee. I sat down and wrote a letter to my mother that night and told her about the series of events that had taken place. I was lost as to what to do next. After I mailed the letter, Popo, Bobby and I got down to the serious business of going through those documents.

16

Preparing for the C.I.D.

I still cannot fathom what the C.I.D. might have been looking for when they eventually searched our apartment. My parents and their politics were well known to the department. I can only surmise that there was someone who may have had a personal vendetta against my father, someone who didn't like him or was envious of him in one way or another. My mother's absence in Nepal didn't help him and was probably used as an excuse to suspect him of being a Chinese spy. As Mr. Lee had explained, Nepal had diplomatic relations with China, whereas India had broken them off. I began to go through my parents' documents. I didn't read or write Chinese but with Popo's help we were able to decipher what was important and what was not—at least we thought we knew. Popo was illiterate but she recognized my parents' handwritings and could identify official-looking documents.

I put the documents into two piles, one for papers that looked important and needed to be hidden, the other for letters that we thought should be destroyed. We spent hours burning letters and flushing the ashes down the toilet just as Mr. Lee had instructed. We did all of this behind closed drapes, with Bobby occasionally peeping from behind the drapes to see if we were being watched. Once, he told us he thought he saw a man hiding behind the bushes. We began to feel nervous.

After burning the letters we went around our flat looking for places to hide the documents that we felt needed to be saved. Bobby wanted to hide some inside the fireplace. We had seen this in an old World War II movie. Our flat had three small old-fashioned, iron-grated fireplaces, one in the living room, and one in each of the bedrooms. On both sides of the firebox there were recessed areas where one could hide things. I thought it was a great idea and we started putting some of the documents in there.

Then I got to thinking, "You know, Bobby, if we had seen this in the movies then the C.I.D. people must know about it too and they will search there for sure."

"Yeah, you're probably right," he agreed but was disappointed we couldn't use the idea.

"Let's put some of the documents in Lassie's bed," I said. "You know how upset he gets when anyone touches it."

"Okay, that's a good idea, and maybe he'll bite them if they touch his bed," Bobby said gleefully.

Lassie was a wonderful dog and people in town knew him by name. He was a golden Tibetan terrier, had long hair, and stood about eighteen inches high. Everyone loved him including the kids in the neighbourhood. However, he had a few peculiar habits. He loved to chase anything that ran: other dogs, people, and horses. He nipped at their ankles if he could catch up with them. We always warned anyone who was running to slow down and walk if Lassie was around. He also disliked anyone coming near his bed, which was a two-foot-square wooden box, about a foot high. We both agreed it would be safe to put documents under his bedding.

We hid the rest of the documents under the living room carpet. We moved the furniture aside, rolled the carpet half way, put the documents in the middle, and then rolled the carpet back over them. We tidied up the house and felt we had done our best and were ready for the C.I.D. if they ever came. It was a tense process because we knew that if we failed, we would put our father in jeopardy.

17

A Visit from the C.I.D.

Mid-morning a few days after we hid and burned the letters and documents, there was again a knock on the front door. Sailee opened it to three men who announced they were from the C.I.D. They said they needed to come in and search the house. I recognized one of them—the person in charge—as a friend of my father's.

"Hello," he greeted us when he caught my eye, and tried to be as pleasant as possible. "How are you all doing?"

"Not too well," I told him, "I'm sure you know our father is in jail. Why was he taken away? We haven't seen him for such a long time. When is he coming home?"

"I know your father well. We have been friends for a long time. It's just that the war between India and China has made things complicated. Tell me, why did your mother go to Nepal?"

"I don't know. She left when I was still in boarding school, but she's coming back soon."

"If you don't mind, we have to do our job and search around your flat."

"What are you looking for?" I asked.

"Oh, we just have to look for certain things to make sure everything is all right. It won't take long."

"Yes, of course," I nodded.

As they searched the flat, I became anxious, especially when I saw that one of the men was checking the toilet and may have noticed a bit of ash on the floor. He didn't say anything but I worried that he might be growing suspicious. They searched the trash bins in the kitchen and found nothing. Thank goodness we didn't throw any paper trash in there. Then they went into the living room. The first place they checked was the fireplace. I could see Bobby was relieved we had removed everything from our initial hiding place. I was getting increasingly agitated when one of the men—the most officious—went to check the dog's bed. Just minutes before, I had ordered Lassie to get into his bed. He seemed to sense our anxiety and, of course, started growling when the C.I.D. officer approached.

"Oh, please don't disturb the dog. He doesn't like anyone to disturb him when he's in his bed and he will bite you," I warned the agent.

"Then you get the dog out!" He told me roughly.

"No," I yelled back. "He will bite me too. He is sick and I won't move him!"

The moment I let out those words, I regretted my outburst. The good agent, my father's friend, quickly came to my rescue.

"My dear, how old are you now?" he asked me.

I turned thirteen last month," I replied.

"Oh, leave her alone," he said to the nasty agent. "She's only thirteen and she's upset about her father being taken away. Come on, we've seen enough, let's go."

Then he turned to me and said sympathetically, "I know it's all been rather hard on all of you these past few weeks. I will try to do everything I can to help your father."

I thanked him, and Sailee led the three men to the door. As soon as they left, we all went into the living room and flopped down on the sofa, relieved they didn't search further. Popo scolded me for losing my temper. She said I was lucky that my father's friend was there; otherwise we might have been in serious trouble.

The next day Mr. Lee came to the house and we told him what had transpired. "Well, thank goodness they didn't find anything but they might come back," he said. That wasn't very reassuring.

A week went by before I received a reply to the letter I had sent my mother. She was extremely upset when she found out what had happened to our father and was afraid for the rest of us. She had gone out of her way to seek help from the Third Prince of Nepal, who had become a good friend. (She told me later that he was the person who had persuaded her to go to Nepal and open a Chinese restaurant. She had met him at Lighthouse Restaurant in Calcutta. He was there as a patron and he had been impressed with the food. He told her there were no Chinese restaurants in Kathmandu and it would be great to have one.) As the youngest brother of the King, he was often called the "Third Prince" by the citizens and the foreign community alike.

The Third Prince and the King both had children who attended Loreto Convent and North Point so the palace always sent the King's plane from Kathmandu to pick up the royal children at the end of the school term. Although school had closed and most of the girls had returned home, the

King's plane had been delayed (possibly for some politically motivated reason since Nepal had friendly ties with China). My mother pleaded with the Prince to see if he could get permission from the palace to reserve two seats on the King's plane for Bobby and me so that we could join the royal children on their return home. The Prince immediately contacted the palace and was able to reserve the seats.

In her letter to me, my mother gave me strict instructions on what to do. She told me the King's plane was coming in a few days to pick up the royal children and take them home. She gave me the place, the date and time of the plane's departure, and at the bottom of the letter, she stressed in bold underlined print "Darling, you both must be there to catch the plane. It may be the last one to Nepal for a long time so do not miss it! I will be waiting for you at the airport in Kathmandu."

18

Visiting Papa in Jail

When Mr. Lee returned later that day, Popo invited him to join us for tea. He was both pleased and worried when I told him that I had received a letter from my mother.

"Mummy wants us to go to her in Kathmandu and has given me detailed instructions on what to do." I discussed the letter in detail.

He thought for a moment and replied. "You are lucky to have such a loving and capable mother, but I must advise you that if you both leave, it may have negative implications for your father. He is already under suspicion of being a spy and this would give his enemies ammunition to build their case. You should think this over seriously before you make any decision." The anticipation and joy of seeing our mother was dashed.

Mr. Lee followed up with better news: he had been able to get permission for us to visit Papa in jail. This time he accompanied us with the proper documents in hand. We were so excited at the prospect of seeing our father. It was the longest three weeks!

When we arrived at the jail, the authorities informed us that only one person was allowed inside. Because I was the oldest, I was chosen. I remember that visit clearly. I was so happy to see Papa, but he seemed drawn, so much older, and he had lost a lot of weight. He was happy to see me too. There were four men sitting at the back of the room who had no intention of leaving us alone. I looked at them and then back at my father with a puzzled expression.

"Those men are interpreters," Papa explained to me. "One speaks Tibetan; the second, Nepali; the third, Chinese; and the fourth, English. You must be a very important person since you have so many interpreters present," he joked.

I was annoyed that I couldn't speak to Papa alone, but then I realized that by pointing out the interpreters, he was warning me that I should be careful about what I said.

"How are you all doing?" he asked me. "How are Popo and Bobby? I'm sorry I was not able to return home that day they took me to jail. They told me they wanted to ask me a few questions down at the jail but when I arrived they just locked me up without any explanation. They sent a Tibetan man because I trust Tibetans and somehow they knew that. They tricked me. Now they are accusing me of being a spy for China. Can you imagine that! It is so ridiculous! Those people at C.I.D. know me very well and they know how I feel towards the Communist Chinese, but they refuse to listen to what I've said."

"Papa, we're managing all right. Don't worry about us. We miss you so much and wish you could come home.

Bobby is waiting outside because they only allowed me to see you. Both of us have been coming every day to bring you food and, of course, Sailee accompanies us. Popo is getting very nervous about what's happening. We have heard from Mr. Lee and others that Chinese are being arrested and taken away in the middle of the night. By the way, Papa, do you know Mr. Lee? He just turned up and is the only one helping us."

"Yes, I know him. He owns a shoe shop in the bazaar and is quite successful. He's a nice young man. Your mummy and I have done a lot for the Chinese community so I'm not surprised that he came to help."

"I received a letter from mummy the other day and she wants us to spend winter holidays with her like last year. She has reserved two seats on the King's plane for us and we have strict orders from her to be on that plane."

"I agree with your mummy totally. You should listen to her and follow her instructions."

"What about you, Papa?" I said. "We cannot just leave you here in jail. We don't know what's going to happen to you and also, we cannot leave Popo all by herself. You know she doesn't speak Hindi or English and I think she would feel very lost and confused if we suddenly left her alone. I know Sailee will look after her until you are released but I don't think it's a good idea to leave her."

"Darling," he looked at me intently, and then continued in a soft voice, "I think your mother is right. You both should join her. This may be the last opportunity for you to travel there without hardship. I'm sure Popo can look after herself, and I will be out of here soon and will take care of her. Don't worry about us."

"Okay. I hope Mr. Lee can arrange for us to have another meeting soon. Oh, we recently went to see to your best friend, and then Mother Superior, to ask for their help. Mother Superior said she couldn't help us because it was a political matter, but I was most astonished when Uncle closed the door in my face. He said he couldn't do anything to help either. I thought he was your best friend, Papa."

"I understand that. They are worried about getting into trouble themselves. I don't blame them for being scared. Things have changed a lot lately."

The rest of the conversation turned to mundane things until the guard signalled that the visit was over. Papa gave me a big, intense hug and whispered in my ear, "Darling, go to Mummy!" Before I left the visiting room, I turned again and looked at him. We both had tears welling up in our eyes. It was sad leaving him since we both had no idea when we would see each other again.

On the way home, Bobby asked me, "So, how was Papa? How did he look? When is he coming home?"

I told him that Papa looked really thin and sad. He has no idea when he'll be coming home. He said that we should follow Mummy's instructions and take the plane to Kathmandu. "You know, I feel really bad about just leaving him when he is in jail. We have no clue what will happen to him." I said. "Besides, I also feel bad leaving Popo behind in Darjeeling by herself."

"I miss Mummy so much and want to be with her," Bobby said. He continued, "We probably shouldn't go to Nepal. I also think we shouldn't leave Popo by herself." I remember how sad and disconsolate my little brother looked as we both wrangled with the decision of whether to go to Nepal to be with our mother, or stay to protect my father and grandmother.

That night I couldn't sleep. The visit with Papa and his strong plea to follow my mother's instructions kept replaying in my head. I knew he wasn't thinking about himself, he just wanted his children to be safe. My father had looked so sad and tired in the jail cell, and I couldn't bear leaving him behind, not knowing what might happen to him. Would they keep him there forever because we left the country? Or worse, might they kill him? If so, it would be my fault because I would have given his enemies a pretext to do so.

On the other hand, if we decided not to go to Kathmandu, Mummy would be so upset she could have a heart attack. She was prone to having heart attacks, or at least that's what everyone called them. She usually recovered by taking one of her tiny pills. Maybe this time the shock would be too great, she might not recover and then it would be my fault too and I couldn't live with that. I tossed and turned all night, not knowing what to do.

The following day Bobby asked if I had made up my mind. I tried to explain the strange phenomenon of our mother's heart attacks. "You know what will happen when Mummy doesn't see us coming off the plane. She's going to have a heart attack."

"What do you mean? Why does she do that?"

"I really don't know. All I know is that if she gets too angry or too excited, she passes out. Sometimes if she gets too hot, she also passes out. For this purpose she keeps these tiny little pills, her heart pills, in her handbag. When she feels faint, she pops one of those pills into her mouth and then she's fine again." I told Bobby about one time when this happened.

She had taken me to the bazaar to do the marketing for the restaurant. It was a warm day and we were coming out of the meat market. She just finished haggling over the prices when, all of a sudden, she said she was feeling faint and sat down on the ground. She told me to quickly open her handbag and find her heart pill in a little brown bottle. I was terrified and started panicking because I had trouble finding it. I finally found it and popped the pill into her mouth. After a few moments, she was okay again. Of course, by the time she was on her feet a crowd of people had surrounded us. They were very concerned about her but happy to see her recover so quickly. It was scary. I was afraid this could happen if she didn't see us coming off the plane.

"Then we must go to her. I don't want her to have a heart attack!" Bobby said looking worried.

We were thirteen and eight and trying to decide whether we should get on the plane to Kathmandu to safety and be reunited with our mother but face the possibility of losing our father forever; or, remain in Darjeeling with Popo and cause our mother to have a heart attack. We weighed the pros and cons, trying to make the most difficult decision of our lives. In the end, we decided to remain in Darjeeling. We thought Mummy would most likely recover by taking her medication, but our departure would mean a worse outcome for Papa. We had no idea what the people in power might do to him. Popo had encouraged us to go to our mother but we reassured her that we would not abandon her. I think she was quietly relieved.

19

The Midnight Knock

Days after we decided not to travel to Nepal, there was another knock on the door. We had just finished dinner and were cleaning up. We froze. I took my time to answer it. When I finally did, there was a young man standing there. He was Nepali, dressed Western-style in a pair of trousers and a sweater, probably in his late teens or early twenties. He appeared nervous and spoke rapidly. He told me that he had been sent to inform us that the two seats reserved for us on the royal plane were no longer available and we should not attempt to go to the airport. He made no eye contact, just delivered the message and took off as fast as he could before I could even question or challenge him. I was furious. I knew he was lying. He, or someone else, must have found out about our two seats and wanted them. Even though we had decided not to go to Nepal, I felt that he should have had the decency to ask whether we were going to use them or not. I was annoyed about this for a long time.

The next week and a half moved slowly as we made our

daily trek down and back from the Darjeeling jail. We kept our drapes drawn and played games in the house, never venturing out. Following Mr. Lee's advice, Bobby stopped going out to play with his friends in the street and most of our Indian friends stopped coming by to visit. He told me that he did sneak out once but came back quickly because one of his schoolmates started saying hurtful things to him.

"What did they say?" I asked.

"They kept chanting, 'Ching Chong, Chinaman, Ching Chong, Chinaman'. What does that mean?"

"I don't know," I replied. "That happened to me once too, shortly before school ended. One of my best friends said that to me out of the blue and started laughing. I was very hurt because I had never heard anything like it before and didn't understand why she said it. I'm sorry that happened to you too but I know how you feel."

In the end, we had only one friend who still came to see us. She was the same Chinese girl I had met in Mother Dolores' elocution class during the last year in school. She was the younger of the two sisters I sat with at the back of the classroom. She and I became close when I became a day scholar and even closer after school ended. She dropped by our house frequently when Papa was home and often stayed for dinner. After Papa was taken away she brought us news about the Chinese community, usually bad news.

She told us things like, "You know, Mr. Wang was taken away last night, and a couple of nights before that, Mr. Chen disappeared. Do you know what happens? The police come to someone's house in the middle of the night and knock on the door; the next thing you know, the father, or husband, or uncle, disappears. No one knows where they are taken. The

Chinese in the community are getting nervous and dreading the 'midnight knock'."

We felt vulnerable as well. Popo started talking about how maybe our turn would come soon. In subsequent days, living in this uncertain, tense atmosphere, we started to suspect our days were numbered.

Mr. Lee visited every one or two days. He had been a godsend ever since my father was arrested, almost a month now. He told us glumly that Papa was going to be kept in jail indefinitely. He had also heard rumours that the three of us, Popo, Bobby and me were all on the list to be taken soon. He didn't know how soon, but he said it could be any day and that we should be prepared to leave at a moment's notice. After we heard that, we became even more anxious. We knew now, without doubt, we would be taken away soon.

A day or two later, three Indian police officers showed up. They drove right up to Ajit Mansion in their military jeep. Since cars were not allowed into the Chowrasta area, the vehicle drew attention. We heard the commotion and peeked out the window. People crowded excitedly around the jeep to see why it was there. One officer remained with the jeep while the other two came up to our flat. They were in khaki uniforms and appeared unemotional. They told us they had come to take us away and that we should be prepared to be away for a long time. They didn't take kindly to our questions and answered brusquely. They didn't know where we were being taken or how long we would be gone. We needed to take warm clothes, bedding, a few pots and pans, and other essentials needed to exist for many months. We were allowed to take one bag each and then they told us they would be back in an hour.

There were so many things to consider. First and foremost in my mind was Lassie. He was my best friend. I was worried about what would happen to him after we were gone.

"What about my dog? Can I please take my dog with us?" I had asked the officer in charge.

"Of course not, don't be ridiculous!" he snapped.

What about Sailee? What was going to happen to her? I looked at her and I could tell she couldn't believe what she was seeing. We hugged and both started crying. With tears streaming down, she told us not to worry, that she would be all right and would take care of Lassie and our house until we returned.

Popo took care of packing Bobby's and her own personal things and I took care of mine. I was sure she would pack her foot care items so that she could take care of her bound feet while away. She packed our bedding and a few pots and pans and I don't remember much else. When we were going through our parents' file cabinet—following Mr. Lee's instructions to destroy or hide papers—we came across a dozen or so men's Rolex and Omega watches among other items left over from Papa's import-export business. I was fascinated by them and wanted one. For some reason, I thought they might come in handy so I picked three of the smallest Omega watches, one for Popo, Bobby and myself, and then I put a Rolex watch in my suitcase to give Papa when we met him again. I don't remember what items I packed for myself, other than books, pens, pencils and a fork-and-knife set. I remembered to take sanitary napkins since I just had my first period. I only packed one month's supply since I didn't think that far into the future. (In fact, I never did use them. It was only later that I realized that my period had stopped for four or five months.) We packed some things for my father because when he was arrested a month before, he had left with just the clothes on his back.

While we were packing, I asked Sailee to go down to the bazaar to look for Mr. Lee and tell him what was happening. Minutes later, she returned with him. It was such a relief to see him. He was apologetic when he realized what was happening and was helpless to do anything to prevent it. We reassured him it was not his fault. He had tried hard to help us. He told Popo that he would take care of things while we were away and make sure that both Sailee and Lassie were taken care of. Many things went through my mind. What have we done? Where are they taking us? Maybe we'll see our father in jail. I was glad my mother was not there though I missed her terribly.

The officers returned shortly after Mr. Lee arrived. They helped us carry our things down to the waiting jeep. By now there were a few dozen curious people surrounding the jeep. They watched as we got into the vehicle. I don't know what they were thinking. I had the feeling they were in disbelief and wondering why we were being taken away. My parents had been in India for over twenty years and were a vital part of the community. They ran a successful and popular restaurant, were liked and respected. Both my brother and I were born in India. Weren't we Indians? Why were we being treated differently? What had we done?

We said goodbye to Mr. Lee and thanked him for everything he had been able to do on our behalf. He looked forlorn standing there as we climbed into the jeep.

I looked at our neighbours who were watching us being carted off like common criminals: a grandmother with bound feet, her thirteen-year-old granddaughter and her eight-year-old grandson. They didn't look at us as old friends and neighbours. It was a different look, one of astonishment. It also seemed to say we were outsiders. A flood of simultaneous emotions overwhelmed me: bewilderment, fear of the unknown, and a feeling of shame: shame for being Chinese.

20

Darjeeling Jail

We were driven down the very road we had walked on every day for the past month. The jeep arrived at Darjeeling jail. This time we were hustled in instead of having to wait outside while our food was delivered to our father. We were surprised to see dozens of other Chinese people already there, waiting in long lines, including entire families: parents, grandparents and children. As I watched, I noticed that once the families were checked in at the table, the men and the women were separated, men through a door on the left, and women through the door on the right. It suddenly dawned on me that because of my short hair and somewhat unfeminine attire, I was probably going to be sent through the men's door. I was horrified and started panicking, "Popo, Popo, you must tell them I'm a girl, tell them I'm a girl!" At first she had no idea what overcame me but then she looked in the direction I was looking and realized why.

There is an explanation for my fear. As I mentioned before, I had become a big fan of Enid Blyton's Famous

Five series. George was my heroine and I wanted to be just like her. Just before my mother left town, two years prior to our arrest, I asked her if she would cut my hair really short, like a boy's. I also asked if she would have trousers made for me. She was curious about this sudden request so I merely told her it was the new style. After that, I wore pants all the time and was always pleased when people mistook me for a boy. Now, it seemed possible this could backfire and my mistaken identity would get me sent to the men's side of the jail.

As we stood in front of the check-in table, the man in charge, predictably, started to send me through the men's door. I held on to Popo's arm tightly. In her mixture of Chinese and Hindi, mostly Chinese, she said, "She's not a boy, she's a girl. You must not send her in there." The man looked at me skeptically but still tried to make me go through the men's door. Still holding on to Popo's arm very tightly, I shouted in Hindi, "I'm not a boy!"

Several women and girls, who had already been checked through and were waiting nearby, had been observing the commotion. When they heard me shout they realized that I was a girl so they backed us up and all started shouting in Hindi, "She's a girl! She's a girl!"

Finally, after several minutes of shouting and crying, pushing and pulling, the man relented and motioned for me to go with my grandmother. Since Bobby was only eight he was automatically allowed to go in with us. There were many other little boys there as well. If the boys looked to be adolescents or teenagers, they were sent to the men's side. I did not leave my grandmother's side for the rest of the evening.

* * *

There were about fifty or sixty women and children in one large room. We were each given army blankets and told to sleep on the concrete floor. We didn't get any food or water but no one seemed to care. It had been a long and trying day and we were all emotionally and physically exhausted. All we wanted to do was to lie down on the floor and go to sleep. I fell asleep quickly.

The next day after the sun came up, we were herded into an open courtyard. It was good to see the daylight but when we looked around we realized that we were indeed in a prison. The compound was surrounded by high walls. In one corner, there was a watchtower and a guard on duty. Only by standing in the middle of the courtyard could one see the boundary of the botanical gardens on the hill outside the walls. I thought I saw Sailee coming down to see us with Lassie. Maybe she came hoping to get a glimpse of us. I waved frantically and got Bobby to wave as well. We thought she waved back, but it was probably my imagination; after all, I believed that she did not know where we had been taken.

Bobby and I went looking for a bathroom and found two, filthy, Indian squat-style toilets. I had always been squeamish about Indian toilets and these were particularly grungy. We hadn't had anything to eat or drink since leaving home, so, luckily, we didn't have need to use them often. Shortly after we were all outside, there was a big commotion at the centre of the compound. We saw dozens of men and women lining up to get breakfast. They turned out to be the same group that had been arrested the day before. Families that were separated the night before were reunited in the courtyard. Popo told us that we should get something to eat. We got in line, and when we finally reached the tables where food was being dished out, we saw three men plopping ladlefuls of some awful-looking, bad-smelling gruel from a huge cauldron into whatever container we could get our hands on. We had nothing with us so a man who had finished eating gave us his large tin can lid. The jail attendant plopped some gruel onto it and we carried it back to Popo. Bobby was enthusiastic about trying it. I looked at him in disgust and couldn't believe he liked it. I refused to eat. It smelled and looked so awful, it made me want to puke.

"Kuai Kuai, you should eat a little," Popo tried to coax me again, using the Chinese term of endearment. "You don't know when our next meal will be."

"I would rather starve to death than eat that stuff!" I told her with indignation. "That looks like slop for pigs."

To set an example, she put on a brave front and tried eating the gruel. She could barely eat it. Only Bobby didn't seem to mind. After he filled his tummy, he went off to explore the rest of the jail grounds.

When he returned he told me, "I visited a couple of prisoners and I think they are mad, especially this one woman. She stares at people with such crazy eyes, and acts just like a wild animal. I was near her cell when some of the big boys started teasing her and making fun of her."

"That was mean, why did they do that?" I asked him.

"I guess just to see her get angry. When she got angry she pounced on her window bars like a wild animal and started throwing her poo at the boys. This made them laugh and tease her even more. After a while they got bored and left her alone so I went up to her and sat quietly outside her cell."

"You sat outside her cell? Weren't you afraid she'd throw poo at you too?"

"No. By the time I came up to her cell she looked exhausted and had calmed down so I just sat outside her window and looked at her. I felt sorry for her. After a while she started talking to me. We talked for several minutes. It seemed like she just wanted someone to listen to her and so I listened."

Papa told us afterwards that many of the inmates were mentally ill and should have been in a hospital rather than in jail. He told us the story about his cellmate, a Bengali tailor, put in jail because he was accused of stealing the clothes he had made for a client. One of his customers had ordered a suit and given him a little money to get started. After completing it, he took the suit back to his customer who refused to pay him the balance and, instead, accused him of taking too long. The tailor became enraged; he needed the money to feed his family. He took the suit back again and sold it to someone else. Then, his customer reported him to the police; the tailor was arrested and thrown in jail.

By the time Papa was imprisoned, the tailor had been there for three years without hope of ever being released. He was becoming crazy. Papa told us that when he was first locked up, the tailor picked grass and white flowers from the yard and offered them to my father. Another time he poured cold water on Papa's head. Papa reacted angrily at first, but after the prison guard told him his story he felt sorry for him. The guard also explained that the tailor had never seen a Chinese person before and so he thought my father was some sort of god; that was why, in his own mind, he was making an offering. Papa shook his head and said the government was just hopeless. The tailor was one of the cellmates with whom my father had shared the food we had brought to him.

After breakfast we heard conflicting reports that circled among the people mulling about the courtyard. One suggested that the prison authorities were getting ready to relocate us to another prison; another was that we were going to remain in Darjeeling jail indefinitely; still another rumour was that those of us who had relatives taken away weeks earlier would soon be reunited. About mid-afternoon there was a different kind of buzz in the air. People were excited about something. As we tried to find out the cause, we saw new people among us. Then, there he was, standing in front us: Papa had been released out to the courtyard and had found us.

"The prison guard informed me and others already in jail this morning that there were many new prisoners brought in last night. He told me that members of my family might be among them and that's why I came looking for you. I hoped I would not find you all. I'm sorry you decided not to follow your Mummy's instructions and now you are in jail too."

"Papa, we really wanted to go to Mummy but we felt we just couldn't go to Nepal and leave you here and Popo by herself at home. Don't feel bad. We are happy now that we are finally together again." He was moved by our decision even though he felt it was the wrong one.

He gave us big hugs. For the first few moments the three of us forgot we were in jail, we were so happy to be reunited. We suddenly remembered Popo and immediately went to look for her. Amid the confusion and excitement, we found her sitting calmly meditating on a bench in the shade. She was so relieved to see Papa and I also felt a great relief as if a heavy weight had been lifted off my shoulders. He was now there to make the decisions and I could go off and play. Well, not exactly play, but at least I could join Bobby in investigating the jail. He was anxious to show me all that he had discovered that morning, including the mad woman.

The rest of that day, we told our father everything that had happened since his arrest. Again he expressed his regret that we had missed the opportunity to leave India to join our mother, but we could see how moved he was that we had given it up to stay with Popo and protect him. I told him how helpful Mr. Lee had been—the only person to come to our aid. Papa then told us the latest rumour he heard from the prison guards the previous evening: it was that all the Chinese people in jail would be relocated that very day. No one knew where we would be taken.

21

Train to Rajasthan

At dusk, the Chinese prisoners were assembled in the courtyard. The head jailer announced that we would be leaving shortly in several army trucks and taken to Siliguri Train Station. He instructed all families to stay together. We queued up for a long time and it was already dark when the prisoners were assigned to various trucks. When our turn came, we were loaded onto a covered military truck along with a couple of other families. I was thankful that Papa was with us. It would have been difficult for my brother and me to load our belongings onto the truck by ourselves.

It was dark when the signal was given to get the convoy moving. There must have been fifteen or twenty trucks, but due to the darkness it was difficult to be certain. There was much confusion because I don't think the Darjeeling prison authority had ever undertaken this kind of mass transfer. The convoy started up the hill from the jail through the bazaar, and onto the road to Siliguri.

On the way down to the train station, the convoy stopped

in Kurseong, a district south of Darjeeling, and picked up more families. One family that boarded our truck brought large amounts of food with them, including a big sack of rice, pots and pans, and a kerosene stove. They somehow knew we were being sent to a faraway place for a very long time and came well prepared.

Three hours later, we arrived at Siliguri Train Station where we were told to wait on the platform before receiving instructions to board. As we waited, we noticed that there were hundreds more people waiting with us than there had been at the jail. First, we were directed to one platform and no sooner had we arrived there, we were told to go to another. Nobody in charge seemed to know what to do. Orders changed just as soon as they were issued. Many people, including us, assumed that we were being sent to a larger prison in or near Calcutta.

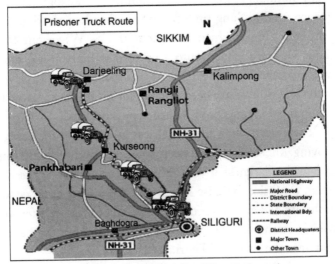

Our convoy from Darjeeing jail to Siliguri train station

I had no idea what time it was when we finally got assigned to a compartment. Our family stuck together like glue. We didn't want to be separated again. Although all the families had boarded, we were still kept waiting for hours at the station. Later, we found out that the delay was caused by the arrival of over a thousand prisoners from border regions of Assam. Those of us who had been waiting at the platform were from districts of West Bengal and were mostly from Darjeeling, Kalimpong, and Kurseong. Our numbers were far less than those joining us from the Assam region. It appeared that people from these regions were shepherded onto compartments near each other. In the wee hours of the morning the train finally started to move. We were all so exhausted from the events of the previous forty-eight hours that by the time the train started, it was such a relief to hear the wheels rolling on the tracks even though we had no idea where we were being taken. I don't know about anyone else but I fell asleep immediately.

When I awoke it was mid-afternoon the next day. I was starving, not having eaten anything since we left home. I looked around the train compartment and saw that it was jammed with people in different stages of sleeping and wakefulness. For the first time I realized that we were all Chinese. I had never been with so many Chinese people before. It was a strange feeling.

There were entire families—mothers, fathers, grandparents, children and grandchildren. I looked out the window as the train whooshed by unfamiliar scenery. Bobby was fast asleep near Popo but Papa was nowhere in sight. I looked at Popo and before I could ask, she read my mind and told me he went to speak with other prisoners. He hadn't talked to any

Chinese people since he was arrested and was eager to find out what they knew. I told her I was starving and she assured me that we would be getting food soon.

Towards evening, Papa returned with some parathas, distributed by the train attendants. Shortly after that they began distributing tea. I was about to wake Bobby but he had already been wakened by the smell of food. We gobbled up the fried bread and wanted more but it was being rationed. We had to make do with one paratha each. I remember how good it tasted. It was probably because we were starving. We drank the tea but it tasted like dirty dishwater. At least it was liquid. For the next couple of days we lived on paratha and dishwater tea. Poor Popo. She had a hard time eating the fried bread. Not only was she not used to eating that type of food, she had false teeth, which made it difficult for her to chew.

On the second day, we noticed that whenever the train stopped at the stations, some of our compartment-mates would hurry to the windows. At first we didn't know why, but it didn't take long to see that they were buying food through the barred windows from vendors on the platform. They had quickly realized that we were not going to be given much food. Following their example, we started doing the same. We were fortunate Popo had brought some money with her, although I don't know how much.

At each station stop, we heard the vendors shouting out their wares: "*Garam chai, chai garam; pakora, andha puri.*" They were the tastiest snacks ever. The tea was just as good. However, as more people on the train found out they could buy food from the vendors, there was a rush to the windows when the train pulled up. Within minutes all the food was sold out. The paratha and tea distributed on the train, and whatever we were able to buy from station vendors, sustained us for the following four days. On the second day, in the next compartment, Papa found a family cooking congee on their one-burner kerosene stove. He asked if they could spare a bowl of congee for Popo because she could not eat the fried bread. They were sympathetic and generously brought her a bowl of rice whenever they cooked it. Popo was grateful.

Armed guards were posted on the platform at every station, as well as at each compartment exit. The guards were Indian, always dressed in their khaki uniforms. After the last load of prisoners boarded the train in Siliguri we never saw anyone get on or off the train, so Papa and the other adults concluded that it was a special train for us.

It must have been quite a sight for the Indian passengers on the platforms to see a whole trainload of Chinese escorted by armed guards. I have often wondered what they thought when they saw us. Later, Papa concluded the reason we stopped at each station (even though no one got on or off) was so that the Indian government could show its citizens that it was punishing the Chinese for invading India by carting them away to prison.

After travelling for more than two days everyone arrived at the same conclusion: we were not going to Calcutta. We used to take the overnight train from Siliguri to Calcutta and at this point we had already spent two nights on the train. People began to speculate as to where we were being taken but no one had any idea. For the remainder of the journey, we stared out of the window at the countryside rushing by, wondering why our lives had suddenly taken such a drastic turn. Some of the adults tried to get to know one another and exchanged stories about how and when each was arrested, while others just slept. Some of the older children played games while most of the younger ones stuck close to their parents or grandparents. Throughout the journey, Bobby and I stayed close to Popo.

22

Camp Deoli

By late afternoon of the fourth day, the train came to a final stop. It sat on the platform for hours. It was already dusk before we were ordered to get off the train and onto trucks again, and night had long fallen before our convoy arrived at our destination. We were ordered off the trucks and told to wait again. We disembarked. It felt good to be on firm ground. I looked around and saw that we were inside a large enclosure, like a military compound. It was surrounded by high barbed-wire fence. We looked at one another, then at those who travelled with us in the same compartment, and finally at those further away. It was the same expression on everyone's face, one of amazement and disbelief. Hundreds of people were standing around looking bewildered and dazed. Eventually we learned that we were among the 2,500 Chinese who had been picked up from India's border regions and brought to this camp.

A military commandant was standing on a platform above us all. "Welcome to the state of Rajasthan," He announced.

Rajasthan? We had no idea where that was. Our father explained that we were in western India, several hours from New Delhi by train or car, over a thousand miles from home. We could not believe that we had been taken so far away from home, across almost the entire expanse of India. People around us, overhearing my father's explanation began asking similar questions. Why were we sent so far away from home? What had we done? What heinous crimes had we committed? Everyone became angry. What sort of injustice was this?

None of us had been given the opportunity to tell our friends or relatives where we were going. We had all been kept in the dark, and now no one would be able to find us. The announcement stirred up quite a hubbub. Some people were shouting, "Let's fight back!" Others raised their fists but we had nothing to fight with. My father tried to calm those around us, "Let us hear what the Commandant has to say."

Everyone finally quieted down and the Commandant started once again to welcome us. He explained that we were brought there by the authority of the Indian government because of the war between India and China. We had been particularly selected because we lived in the border areas. He told us that he didn't know how long we would be kept there but that we would be treated well as long as we did not attempt to escape. He said any attempt to escape would be futile since we were in a desert, miles from civilization. He said that he was sure that after the war was over we would be able to return home.

He then proceeded to give us instructions. We had to go through a brief interrogation and give our names and addresses. After that we would be assigned accommodation where we would remain until released. They were going to

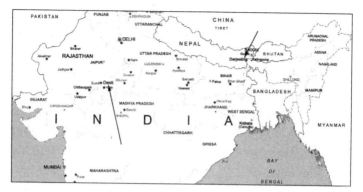

Map of our train journey

confiscate all sharp objects, particularly knives and scissors, for our own safety and take our cash for safekeeping. He said we would receive a form on which we should state the amount of money and other personal items we had brought with us, and they would be returned to us upon departure. He thanked us for our cooperation and again welcomed us to Deoli.

As we waited in the long queues to be checked in, people began questioning the Indian government's logic. After all, we were ordinary people who just happened to be living on the border. Most of us were either born in India or had lived in India for decades. Most of us were not China sympathizers. While these debates were going on, I watched men and women being ushered into inspection rooms located off the sides of the fenced yard in a small concrete building with a corrugated tin roof. Those who went through the interrogation and returned told us what to expect. They explained that only the head of the household had to fill out the forms, including the names of all accompanying family members and the amount of cash or jewelry that was being taken by the guards for safekeeping.

I watched as people came and went from the makeshift inspection room. Each person took in his or her possessions to be inspected. When they came out they brought their belongings with them and rejoined their families who were waiting outside. Younger children were told to accompany an adult. After the inspection, people proceeded to another line where they were assigned a sub-camp for their living quarters. There were four sub-camps and we were assigned to Camp Four.

One of the things I brought with me was my school attaché case, a well-worn brown leather case the size of a briefcase, with my name printed in white on one side. It had served as my weekend bag when I was allowed to go home once a month during my boarding school years. I had my personal belongings in it: pencils, paper, books, a first-aid kit and a knife. I don't remember what else, but I do remember the dinner knife.

As we stood, waiting to be inspected, it turned dark. The grounds were dimly lit, with only a few spotlights scattered throughout the compound, including a searchlight that beamed from a nearby watchtower. Those in our train compartment had been grouped together at one end of the field. I had set my attaché case down a small distance away from us near a tree and had forgotten to take it with me into the inspection room. Papa took Bobby with him into the men's inspection room and I went with Popo into the women's side. When we came out, I noticed that my attaché case was still sitting in the same place. Since it was dark, no one had noticed it. I calmly walked up to it and picked it up feeling very pleased with myself. Bobby looked at me and wondered why I was smiling. As we were waiting to be assigned to our house I whispered to him that I had a knife in my attaché case. He was very excited to learn that we had something that we were not supposed to have. Popo, we learned later, had also sewn some extra money into our clothes to be used "just in case" although we had no idea where or how we would use it.

Unfortunately, we had to give up our precious Rolex and Omega watches. I was sad to see the authorities take them and I regretted having come up with the idea of each of us wearing one in the first place. Bobby and I didn't get our watches back when we left the camp and I doubt if either Papa or Popo's watches were ever returned.

23

Doing Time with Nehru

It was the middle of the night when our group was directed to Camp Four, listed as "Darjeeling camp" because we were all from the Darjeeling district. It was a long walk in the dark from the inspection headquarters. When we got there, each family was instructed to choose a bungalow among thirteen or fourteen similar buildings. All of a sudden, there was a mad dash to pick the best one. At first we had no idea what was happening, but then we realized what others were doing. In the midst of the frenzy, we chose Bungalow No. 2 because it was closest to the gate. Popo was extremely exhausted and could hardly take another step on her little bound feet. All she wanted to do was to sit and put up her poor tired feet. We later learned that Bungalow No. 2 was where Prime Minister Nehru lived when he was interned by the British years before, so we felt very privileged. It felt like we were "doing time with Nehru."

In the days that followed, my father was chosen to be the liaison between Camp Four and the commandant. From his frequent meetings with the commandant he learned that we had been sent to an internment camp located in the desert outside the small town of Deoli, in the state of Rajasthan in Western India. We called it "the Camp," and to this day my brother and I still refer to it as "the Camp." The British had constructed it at the turn of the twentieth century as an internment camp for civilians. Insurgents and rebels, or anyone that the British deemed troublemakers, were interned here. Nehru had been the most famous "guest" of the British. Ironically, Nehru was Prime Minister when the 1962 Sino-Indian War broke out, and the order to intern Chinese was issued.

The camp in Deoli was perfectly suited to be a place to hold Chinese prisoners since it was already an established internment camp. Located in the Rajasthan Desert, Deoli was hours from civilization and any attempt to escape was futile because of the hostile landscape. Since it was situated far from any town, no attention was drawn to it. Most Indians who lived in or around the Deoli area were unaware that the camp existed because prisoners were always transported at night. If they did know anything about the camp, they didn't talk about it.

Well-fortified, the camp had been designed as a high-security detention centre. It had three sets of barbed wire. The outer fence was about twenty feet high; the middle fence consisted of a continuous roll of barbed-wire about five feet in diameter; and the inner fence was about ten to fifteen feet high. Guard towers were located every hundred feet around the perimeter of the grounds. We learned from the camp officers that the guards were instructed to shoot anyone attempting to escape.

* * *

Camp Four, or Darjeeling Camp, was small compared to the other sub-camps. It was at one end of the grounds. It had a number of self-contained bungalows. Camps One, Two and Three were large, with a series of large barrack-type buildings in each one. They were on the opposite side of the grounds from Camp Four, at least a mile away, or so it seemed. Internees arrested from other parts of the border regions, like Assam, were housed in these other camps. When I went exploring with the kids from Camp Four, I noticed that the barracks appeared to be segregated by gender although young children—both boys and girls—were allowed to be with their mothers.

The housing units in the Darjeeling Camp were rectangular buildings constructed out of concrete blocks. Each had two or three units that could house two or three families in relative privacy. For instance, our unit had two bungalows separated by a thick wall about twelve feet high. It didn't go all the way up to the ceiling, but stopped about a foot below. This made it a perfect place for roosting pigeons!

We were in Bungalow No. 2 and another family next door was in Bungalow No. 1, a mirror image of ours. As you came through the door into our bungalow, you entered a small dirt yard. At the left end, there was a shower stall that accommodated a squatting-style toilet. At the other end, in the right-hand corner, opposite the entrance, there was a wood-burning mud stove. From this little yard you entered through an inner doorway into our sleeping quarters, a large room on a mud floor. There were four single military cots in the room with a small table and two chairs. The family in the adjacent bungalow was also a family of four: a father, mother, and their two sons. We discovered in subsequent days that it

Darjeeling Camp 4

was the same family that had joined our truck on the convoy from Darjeeling to Siliguri, the one that came with many provisions.

Two windows in our sleeping quarters looked out onto the bleak compound where barbed-wire fencing was visible around the perimeter. The windows had wooden shutters to keep the extreme heat out during summer months, and the cold wind during the winter. Since the camp was located in the desert, the climate was extreme: very hot during the day, very cold at night. We had arrived at the beginning of December so the weather was still pleasant, mid-sixties to mid-seventies during the day and mid-forties to mid-fifties at night. The cold nights didn't bother us since we came from a cold climate. My father later told us the summers were unbearable as the temperature rose to 118° F during the day and dropped only to the mid-seventies at night.

That first night, we slept soundly since we were totally

exhausted. The following morning we were wakened by gentle coos. For the first time, we became aware of our living conditions. The bungalow had not been used for some time. Everything was covered with dust. Worst of all, the concrete floor was covered with pigeon droppings. Popo was horrified and immediately set us to cleaning the place. It took us most of the morning to make it livable and we discovered, to our delight, that we had cold running water in the shower stall although we had to use buckets or tin cans to flush the toilet.

Later that morning we received word that food was being served at either Camp One or Camp Two. Both were a long distance from our camp. Bobby and I ran to Camp Two to look for the food since it was a little closer. It still took us about fifteen minutes to get there. We were quite hungry as we hadn't had a proper meal since being taken from our

Bungalow 2

home six days prior. By the time we arrived, there was a long line of internees still waiting for food, which had already run out. We were told to return later. Disappointed, we walked back empty-handed to our bungalow. The next time Papa went with us and we were able to bring Popo a ration of chapatti and undercooked dal. In the beginning, the Indian camp cooks didn't know how to gauge the amount of food to cook and the supply always ran out. Also, because they were under pressure to feed hundreds of people still waiting in line, the cooks never allowed enough time for the lentils to become fully cooked. We were fed undercooked dal for the first several meals. Papa also decided we needed to go much earlier in order not to miss out on meals.

In the first two weeks after we had settled, Popo sent us out to look for firewood for the mud stove. She was tired of trying to eat the under-cooked dal and hoped to re-cook it to a softer consistency. The hard lentils always got stuck between her false teeth and gums and caused great irritation. (I remember when I used to come home from school for the holidays, Bobby and I would often take turns to purposely annoy our grandmother; when she got mad at us, she would crunch down on her false teeth and they would chatter against each other. We delighted in hearing the sound of her chattering teeth and would scream with laughter, which made her even madder.) When we first started looking for firewood, there was an abundance of sticks and dead branches on the grounds outside our bungalow and there was no problem collecting wood. But as people from the other houses also started collecting wood, within days there was not a stick to be found.

Our living quarters

By the fourth day, the camp kitchen finally figured out the right amount of food and the right length of time to prepare it. We also got our first ration of meat curry! We were all very excited and rushed back with it as fast as we could. We had not eaten meat since we left home and when Popo dished out the food that evening we couldn't wait to dig in. What a disappointment! The curry was more like thin gruel than stew. We noticed all sorts of stringy and tube-like things floating in it. It seemed that the entire beast, innards and all, was thrown into a large vat and cooked. The bits that looked like real meat were so tough, it was like chewing on old leather. We asked Papa what the tube-like things were and he couldn't say. It was a shock when we found out later that we were being served old camel meat.

After a few meals of this camel meat, people in the camp rebelled. They were incensed. "What is the Indian authority thinking?" they asked each other. "It's bad enough that Chinese don't eat camel meat, but to serve us the entire carcass, innards and all?" It caused quite an uproar and the camp authority became nervous. Apparently, there had been a dilemma in the camp kitchen. The Hindu cooks were vegetarian and did not handle any type of meat at all; the Muslim cooks, of course, refused to handle pork, which was the favourite meat of the Chinese. The camp officials thought camel meat would be a good compromise; besides, camels were large beasts and could feed many hundreds of hungry people. They had not anticipated the Chinese reaction.

Someone in the camp found out that my father spoke English and had had previous dealings with the Indian bureaucracy, so a group of people appointed him as our spokesman. "Tell them we will go on hunger strike if we are served camel meat again." Initially, my father resisted being the spokesman but in the end he accepted the role and asked permission to speak to the Commandant of the camp. He turned out to be the same man who had welcomed us the first day. After the meeting, things got straightened out and the kitchen stopped serving camel meat. His role of spokesman, my father told me later, was the beginning of a great friendship between him and the Commandant.

Shortly after the near hunger strike, my father ran into a man who used to be his chief chef at the "Lighthouse Restaurant," a second Chinese restaurant my parents had opened—this one in Calcutta—shortly after Pu-Chin left for America. They had it only for two or three years and I was never told why they closed it. Running into Chef Liu was a surprise. Liu had sought out my father after he had heard that my family was also interned. It was like a family reunion. He had been a superb chef when he worked for the Lighthouse but my father had to let him go because he had a short and fiery temper. After we closed the Lighthouse Restaurant, we learned that Chef Liu had moved to the state of Assam and our family completely lost touch with him. He was arrested with thousands of others from that region and when we arrived at the camp he had been assigned to Camp Three. He begged my father to help him get transferred to Darjeeling Camp and told us that his life had been threatened. I don't know what the reasons were; Papa speculated that his temper might have gotten Liu into trouble again, and this time with a group who threatened his life. Liu insisted that he needed to be transferred right away. Papa promised to help.

My father spoke with the other families in our camp and came up with a plan whereby the Darjeeling Camp could be in control of its own meals instead of relying on food from the main kitchen served at the other camp sites. He introduced Chef Liu to the group and explained Liu's situation, and that had once worked for him and was an excellent chef. If they agreed, he would ask permission from the Commandant to have Liu transferred to Darjeeling Camp and we would have our own cook. He would also ask the Commandant to have our food rations supplied directly to our camp and we would take responsibility for our own meals. There were about thirteen families in our camp as compared to hundreds in the other camps. He pointed out that it would be advantageous to us since we would no longer have to queue up in long lines for meals every day. Most importantly, he said, we would be eating better. By this time, my father already had had a number of meetings with the Commandant, and he told the group that he found the man to be reasonable. There were some misgivings among a few of the families but in the end they were all convinced it was a good idea. The Commandant granted permission and Chef Liu was transferred.

Immediately, our meals improved. Popo was so pleased. To this day, I still remember Chef Liu's eggplant curry. It was the best!

24

Life at Camp

L ife at camp was relatively mundane. We woke up, washed, got dressed, and had breakfast which consisted of tea and chapatti. One of my chores was to wash the dishes after each meal. We had no dish soap and the only small bar of soap we had was saved for bathing. I had seen village women in Indian movies using ash from their wood stoves to clean their pots and pans. I decided to give it a try. To my surprise it worked well. I was able to get all the dishes spic-and-span.

Later, after I had been released from camp I developed a severe skin disorder on both my hands. Doctors suspected it might have been the result of using ash to wash dishes. My hands continually peeled like the layers of onion skin and I literally had no fingerprints. My mother took me to various doctors and specialists to find a way to stop my hands from peeling. I was prescribed all kinds of ointment, medication, including lathering my hands with lanolin and sleeping with socks on my hands at night. It took years before my hands returned to normal. (I often thought that I should have used this opportunity to get into the world of crime because I would have left no fingerprints behind!)

At first, Bobby was the only one to go out and make friends with the other children. He was gregarious and had no problem making new friends; in fact, for him, being at camp was like being on an extended camping trip in unexplored territory. After being brought up in a convent for nine years, I was extremely shy and didn't know how to talk to or interact with strangers; I stayed inside "our house." Some of the kids thought I was stuck-up because I was a Loreto girl. Papa kept encouraging me to go out and make friends until I finally ventured out and discovered that the other kids were welcoming and friendly.

We became friends with a group of kids that lived nearby our bungalow, often going on explorations of the entire camp. At other times, we just talked or played games like hopscotch or "pickup stones." In pickup stones, each player found his or her own group of five special stones and took turns throwing them. I remember the boys didn't much care to play this game. Whoever's turn it was, she had to throw the stones on the ground, and then select one to be the lead stone. This she would throw into the air trying to pick up one or two other stones before catching the falling stone. If it landed on the ground, she lost her turn. I don't remember the rules of the game any more but there was a certain sequence in picking them up. We played this a lot to pass the time.

Among our newfound friends, there were two boys who had brought slingshots from home. One boy was particularly adept at using it and loved to hunt birds. He once caught a beautiful little blue-green bird with a long tail and we all rushed over to check it out.

"That is the most beautiful bird I have ever seen. How did you manage to catch it without harming it?" I asked him. "What are you going to do with it?"

He looked at me and said, "Here, you can have it."

He handed me the bird, which he had placed inside a little handmade cage, then walked away. I was so taken with his gesture; I didn't know what to say. I had no idea he was going to give it to me. I was suddenly the proud owner of a beautiful bird and my friends were envious. We spent the rest of the day admiring it, wondering what to feed it and what name to give it. As I watched the bird so desperately trying to get out, I began feeling it was wrong to keep it caged, just as we were. I told Bobby and my other friends that I was going to set it free. They thought I was crazy and tried to persuade me to keep it. I had always had different kinds of pet animals growing up—dogs, cats, lamb, fish, even guinea hens—but never a wild bird, especially not one as beautiful. I almost convinced myself that I should keep it but in the end I decided it wasn't right to keep a wild bird caged up.

That evening, against my friends' protests, I set the bird free. It felt good to see it soar into the sky. Later, when the boy who had given me the bird found out what I had done, he stopped speaking to me. I was sorry because he seemed really nice and I would have liked to have been his friend. This incident led me to becoming obsessed with bird-watching and I discovered that there were many beautiful species of birds in Rajasthan. I particularly remember the parrots and the owls. There was one particular owl that I fell in love with; it was light gray in colour, only about nine or ten inches tall

Bobby and his crow

with little pointy ears and a cute catlike face. I wanted to catch this "cat-owl" and dreamt that after I caught it, I would train it to sit on my shoulder as I roamed the grounds of the camp pretending to be the heroine of one of my adventures. Of course, the owl was free to come and go as it pleased. There was plenty of time for daydreaming and I never did catch the owl. In those days of exploration, I forgot about my mother and didn't think of her at all.

After I freed my wild bird, Bobby was keen on catching one of his own. He pleaded with the boy who had made slingshots to teach him how to make one. At first, the boy wasn't thrilled to share his knowledge: he was still angry at me. He soon relented and told Bobby to look for a Y or V-shaped piece of wood and then he would help him make the slingshot. Without delay, Bobby began to look for the right piece of stick. It was not easy to find, but when he did, he immediately took it to the older boy. He must have been a bird shooter long before he came to Deoli because he seemed to have all the knowledge and the materials he needed to make slingshots. Bobby was elated and thanked him. Armed with his new weapon, he ran off happily looking for his first prey. The first bird he hunted down was a crow.

Later that evening Bobby told me: "I saw this old crow and I decided to practice my catapult on him so I followed him for a long time." He grew animated as he told his story: "It was amazing! The crow wouldn't fly away even though he knew I was chasing him. I aimed my slingshot at him and released the stone but I missed him by just one or two feet. He fluttered his wings and flew just far enough away, and then he waited for me to catch up. I couldn't believe it. He watched me as I reloaded my slingshot and the moment I let go of the stone, he flew off again and landed just far enough away that I missed him a second time. Then he waited for me to catch up again. We repeated this sequence over and over and I missed him every time."

"So, what did you do in the end? Did you finally get him?" I asked.

"No. I'm sure he thought I was hopeless. He finally got tired of me chasing him. When I aimed my slingshot for the last time, he didn't budge. He just sat there, fluttered his wings up and down and looked at me in the eye. He seemed to be saying, 'come on and hit me, you little shrimp!' I looked at him, and he looked back at me, and for a moment he looked like a wise old man. I couldn't shoot him. He finally flapped its wings, gave me one last look and flew away. He was such a cheeky crow!"

A month after we were interned, the people of Darjeeling Camp were summoned to the Commandant's headquarters.

Papa took us with him while Popo stayed behind. We were not quite sure why we were asked to go there. As usual, we had to form long queues. When our turn came we were ushered into a building towards a table where there were two or three officers in charge. One told my father that each family was going to be given rations of certain basic items like sugar, salt, tea, eggs, oil, etc., and that they had worked out a formula based on the number of people in a family. We were rationed two and a half eggs a week. At the time, I thought it was strange. I think children under age fourteen only got half an egg each week, older people above sixty got half an egg, so my grandmother got half an egg, and Bobby and I got half an egg each and my father got a whole egg. (In actuality, we received only two eggs per week.) We were then told that we could use the money we had brought with us to buy extra things, like toiletries, from the canteen. We were also informed that the money had to last the entire time we were there, and no one had any idea how long that was going to be.

The family in Bungalow No. 1—the ones who seemed so well prepared for their stay—were Chinese Muslims. It was the first time I had ever met Chinese Muslims. We never spoke to one another while we were travelling in the truck but later, at camp, when we all became familiar with one another, they told us that they were originally from the province of Sinkiang, in Western China near the Soviet border, and had later emigrated to India. When they were arrested in Kurseong, they felt that because they were Muslim, their special needs would most likely be overlooked, so they decided to take care of themselves. Unlike mainstream Chinese, they didn't eat pork and had different hygiene standards. I think that's why they brought so many basic food items. One of the special items they brought with them, which I particularly remembered, was beef suet. I had never known of anyone using this; Chinese use pork fat in much of their cooking.

The family also brought many pots and pans, a single-burner kerosene stove, a hundred-pound bag of rice, sugar, a sack of flour and other things. My father told me much later that the treatment towards this family was quite the reverse from what they had anticipated. They were actually given special privileges because they were Muslim. Even though Rajasthan is mainly a Hindu state, many of the camp officials were Muslim, and they showed special sympathy towards this family.

Our Muslim neighbours were self-reliant, preferring to stick to themselves though they allowed their sons to play with the rest of us at certain times of the day. The older son was a quiet boy of eleven with an even temperament but his six-year-old brother had an aggressive nature. He had a large red birthmark that covered half his face and I think he was something of a pervert. He followed us around and was generally a pest. We all avoided him and ran the other way whenever we saw him approach. After becoming fed up with his obnoxious behaviour, I decided to teach him a lesson; it wasn't difficult to get Bobby to serve as an accomplice. My plan was to save the dal, which Popo usually threw out, and make them into laddoos. This was before we got our own cook. Laddoos are Indian sweets typically made by rolling gram flour and sugar into round balls. We didn't have gram flour or sugar, just undercooked dal.

"Why do you want to save the dal? It's half raw and tastes yucky." Bobby asked me with a disgusted look on his face.

"I want to make them into laddoos and dry them on top of the bathroom wall."

"Why? I thought you hated it too."

"I know, but I'm getting sick and tired of the little boy next door. He is such a pest. I want to get even with him. He always follows us around to annoy us. Do you know that when he's alone with a girl, he pulls his pants down and shows off his penis?"

"Yuck! that's horrible!" Bobby exclaimed. "I thought he was a brat, but I never knew that. I agree, we should teach him a lesson but what are we going to do with the laddoos?"

"Well, I thought that after they're dried, we'll take some of them and pretend to eat them in front of his house. We'll

Laddoos drying on the latrine wall

make it sound like they are so delicious. I'm sure he'll come out and want to have some. We'll force him into giving us some sugar in exchange for them. But, we have to make sure he's home by himself."

"Wow, it would be great if we could get some sugar from the little brat! Do you think he will fall for the trick?"

"I don't know, but we can try."

We spent the whole morning making two inch round balls with all the half-cooked dal that we had saved, and then put them on top of the bathroom wall to dry. When they were completely dried, and after we determined that the boy was alone, we took them outside our house and began to speak loudly to one another.

"Oh, these laddoos are so yummy. Do you want to try one?" I said to Bobby.

"Okay," replied Bobby, taking one. "Umm. They are sooo delicious!"

Just as I anticipated, the little pervert came running out of his house saying, "What have you got, what have you got? Can I have one too?"

"Sure," I replied, and gave him one.

He took a bite and spat it out. "Yuck. This is not very good."

"Not yet," I said. "You have to dip it into a little sugar. I'll show you how to eat it. Go get some sugar."

He ran into his house and brought out a little sugar. We took the sugar from him and both Bobby and I dipped our laddoos into it and pretended to go into ecstasy. He followed our directions, looked a bit skeptical at first but didn't want to contradict us, so took a bite.

"Umm, this is good. Can I have more?"

"We'll give you four if you give us one cup of sugar," I said to him. At first he was hesitant, but we continued to make such a fuss over how good the laddoos were that he was convinced and went back into his house. While he was getting the sugar, I ran back to our bungalow and found an empty tin can and brought it back anticipating our success. We were lucky that his parents and his older brother were still out and he was able to bring out a cup of sugar without trouble. Before he poured the sugar into my tin can he said, "How many laddoos do you have?"

"Oh, about twelve or so, why?"

"Give them all to me and then you can have my sugar."

"What!" I said looking shocked. I didn't want him to change his mind so I said, "Oh, all right, but you know, you're getting a better deal."

He looked very pleased with himself so we ran back to our house and returned with the rest of the laddoos, made the exchange, and immediately returned home before he changed his mind. We were thrilled with the coup we had pulled off and looked forward to having sugar in our tea for the next several days. We were going to share it with Papa and Popo but then decided it was better that they didn't find out.

Evenings were the most difficult time at camp. There was nothing to do. We had few books to read and we read them over and over during the daylight hours. Popo wouldn't allow us to read at night because all we had was a single 40-watt light bulb. She said it would ruin our eyes. In the end, we talked Papa into telling us stories. It didn't take much to persuade him: he loved telling stories, and he was an excellent storyteller. He told us three main stories while we were at camp—his favourites, which soon became our favourites too. They were "The Three Kingdoms", "The Monkey, a Journey to the West," and "Ji Gong, the Mad Monk." These stories, particularly the first two, play a major part in Chinese art, culture, and history although I didn't know it at this time. They are told over and over in Chinese film, theatre, and opera. They were perfect choices because of their epic length and Papa could go on for weeks and months like a one-man show. He brought the stories alive with his wonderful facial expressions and funny dramatic voices. What my brother and I know of these stories today is through our father, and frankly when we see a new film or read new renditions of these classics, they never come up to par!

Papa started telling us these stories under the shade of a big tree just outside our bungalow, usually in the early evenings after supper. The kids in our age group were curious at first about what was going on. One by one they started coming around to listen. At first they were bored but it didn't take long for them to become hooked, just as we were. Later, the storytelling migrated into our bungalow and every evening after dinner, five or six kids would join us. We sat together on our bed to listen to a new episode of the Monkey's adventures, or hear about another battle in the Three Kingdoms. For me, that was the best time of the day. It transported me into a totally different world full of fantasy and adventure. It was the first time in my life that I felt really close to my father.

Life at camp continued like this for the months Bobby and I were there. To keep occupied and fight off boredom, we invented games with the other children and explored the entire camp. As we wandered the grounds through Camps

Two and Three and got further away from our own territory, I observed that our accommodations at Darjeeling Camp were far better than those of the other camps. In our camp, each family was assigned individual bungalows with a toilet and shower. In the other camps, men and women were segregated and lived in large barrack style buildings with several hundred people in each building. They had public toilets and showers and no private cooking facilities. I asked Papa about this. He said he thought it was because India was so entrenched in the caste system, where definite lines were drawn between the different groups of people in society: between upper and lower class, rich and poor, educated and non-educated. He thought the government believed that the people from the Darjeeling district were more affluent and better educated; therefore, they were afforded more privileges.

The other observation I made while exploring the grounds was that the further away we got from our camp, internees began to look less Chinese and more Indian. We learned that most of the people at the other camps were from Assam in northeast India. This was where most of the fighting between Chinese and Indian troops took place. I concluded that these people must have been living in India for several generations and may have been the offspring of mixed marriages. This impression stayed with me for a long time after we left the camp and drove home the point of how arbitrary and unjust the Indian government policies had been.

25

Mother Finally Gets Word

By mid-December, as Christmas time drew near, we had been in camp for six weeks. Even though most of us were not Christians, many celebrated the non-religious aspects of the holiday, exchanging cards and gifts. Of course, at camp, we had no gifts to give each other but at least we wished each other Merry Christmas. The Commandant gave permission for each family to send one Christmas card to someone of our choosing. This act of compassion suddenly brought us back to reality. My mother. My goodness! I had forgotten about her entirely. We had been so engrossed in learning to survive at camp that we didn't think about life outside.

I started to imagine what my mother's reaction must have been when we didn't step off that plane to Kathmandu. Had she been beside herself with worry and anguish? The last time I wrote to her was when I told her Papa had been arrested, and her last letter to us had provided instructions on making our way to the King's plane bound for Kathmandu. Did she have a heart attack when she didn't see us get off that plane?

Did she know where we were and that we were okay? My father was hesitant to send her a card because he didn't want to bring to the attention of the Indian government that she was residing in Nepal, but we desperately wanted to let her know that we were okay.

Then I had an idea. My mother had introduced us to several of her friends when we visited her in Nepal during winter holidays. I remembered one person in particular, an American woman, who worked for the United States Agency for International Development (USAID). She was a good friend of my mother's, having met her at my mother's hair salon. She had her hair done once a week, then visited our home, often staying for dinner. She also invited us to her house and took us on picnics. I had promised to write to her after our last visit and had brought her address with me to camp.

The American woman was called Dottie. I suggested to Papa that we send our Christmas card to her because I was positive she would deliver it to my mother. He thought it was a brilliant idea. We picked a card from the camp store. I wrote, "Merry Christmas, Dottie. Hope you are well. We are doing fine here. Papa, Popo, and Bobby are with me here in a camp in Deoli, Rajasthan, and have been here for the past several weeks. We hope to go home soon. Please give our love to Mung when you see her. Love, Yin-Chin." My mother's other name was Mung, which she started using after she moved to Nepal.

We later learned the scheme worked well. Dottie took the card to my mother as soon as she received it and my mother immediately sprang into action. She used all her contacts and energy to work out a way to get us out of the camp and back to her in Kathmandu. She was relieved to hear of our whereabouts, and had been distraught when we didn't show up at the airport in Kathmandu and had tried to find out why we didn't follow her instructions. She had desperately tried to get word from us. Of course, she never received a reply. She had not heard anything for weeks and then eventually got news from friends in the intelligence business at the American Embassy that Chinese living on the borders between India and China had been rounded up and sent to an internment camp. No one knew where. Since she had no direct word, she assumed the same fate had befallen us. When Dottie brought the card to her, her relief at finally learning where we were must have been tremendous.

Meanwhile, back at the camp, Christmas came and went. Things carried on much the same, with occasional excitement when groups of Chinese of different political persuasion got into fights. I remember once a group of angry men came to our doorstep, shouting and accusing a neighbour of being a Communist sympathizer and threatening to kill him. It was scary listening to the angry mob. They were saying it was people like him who were responsible for getting us all into prison. My father told us to remain inside our house while he went out to see about the hullabaloo. I don't know what happened next but he returned when the mob finally dispersed. He didn't want to talk about it and I never questioned what happened.

One special event added spice to our lives at camp: we were granted permission to buy two live chickens with our limited money. We bought a red one and a black one, both hens. We had not eaten chicken for ages and Popo was excited over the anticipation of having chicken soup. She prepared and cooked the red chicken with great care on our mud stove, and we looked forward to her delicious soup. Unfortunately, the chicken turned out to be bony and tough. Papa decided it would be best if we fattened the other hen first before we ate her. In the interim, however, I got attached to her and she became our pet, replacing Lassie. Soon, the chicken followed us all over the bungalow. We were afraid to let her outside knowing that someone might grab her for their own soup pot. The black hen must have been content living with us because shortly after we got her, she started laying eggs: one egg a day, and I was able to persuade both Papa and Popo not to eat her. After we left camp, Papa told us that the hen somehow got out of our little yard and someone grabbed it. Papa never found out who it was.

26

Guilty Freedom

In mid-February 1963, not long after we got our hens, I was exploring Camp Three with Bobby and our friends when Chef Liu came running up, out of breath, "Thank goodness, I've found you," he said. "Your father wants you to return to your bungalow right away."

We were puzzled and worried and hoped everything was all right. We raced back. By the time we got to our house, we sensed an unusual buzz about the entire camp. People we knew came up to us and said, "You are leaving. You are set free!"

"We are set free? That's wonderful! When are we all going home?"

"No, no, not everyone, only you and your brother," one man said.

"Why only me and my brother? I don't understand, what do you mean? Where's my father?"

"He's with the Commandant right now. He told us to tell you that you must both wait for him here at the house," a second man answered.

As we waited for our father, we could see that people had gathered along the road that led from Darjeeling Camp to the Commandant's office. Finally, our father showed up smiling. "Yin-Chin, Bobby, get your things together, you are both released and are free to join your mummy."

"Papa, I don't understand, why only the two of us? Why not you and Popo as well? What about all the other people?"

"Your mummy was only able to obtain release for the two of you. She has arranged with some friends who live in New Delhi to drive you to their home today, and then tomorrow, they will take you to the airport and put you on the plane to Nepal. Her friends are waiting for you in the Commandant's office right now."

I threw my arms around him, "No, we can't go and leave you and Popo behind," I started crying. "We should all leave together. When will we see you again?"

"Darling, you must leave when you have the chance. Look at all the people who have come to see you leave. Any one of them would give up anything to trade places with you. You must go before the Indian government changes its mind. Popo and I will join you later."

Once more, Bobby and I were placed in an awkward situation. On the one hand, we were excited to realize we were the first two people to be released from the camp; on the other hand, we were leaving Papa and Popo behind. We had no idea when we would see them again. Papa put his best face forward. You could tell he was full of mixed emotions. Popo and I sobbed as we hugged one another goodbye. As we embraced, she said, "You are both very lucky to have such a clever mother. Kuai Kuai, be good always. We won't be seeing each other again."

Papa had to pry Bobby out of Popo's arms. As we walked down that long road for the last time towards the camp exit, I think Bobby must have felt as I did, seeing the faces of all the people looking on with envy and longing, asking themselves why we were set free and not them. I felt so guilty leaving them all behind.

In the Commandant's office, Papa introduced us to Mr. and Mrs. Taylor who were connected with the United States Embassy in New Delhi. They had previously worked in Kathmandu. Mrs. Taylor was a good friend of my mother's and regularly came to her beauty parlour to have her hair done. After learning of our whereabouts and setting the wheels in motion to secure our release, my mother contacted them and asked if they would do her a huge favour. She asked them to go to Deoli to pick us up from the internment camp and put us on a plane for Kathmandu. She said she would send them all the proper documents required for our release.

There was no hesitation on their part—they agreed immediately. It was hard saying goodbye to our father. It didn't seem right to be separated from him yet again, just when I was beginning to feel close. I somehow felt I would never see him or Popo again. Finally, Mr. and Mrs. Taylor told us we had to get on the road before dark, that it was a long drive to their home. They had to pull us away and we followed them, sobbing, as we walked toward their waiting car.

The drive from Deoli to Delhi took about six hours; I don't remember much of it as I slept most of the way, exhausted by all the emotions we had gone through. It was late afternoon, just outside of the city of Jaipur, when we stopped to fill the car with gasoline and have a snack. Most of the drive after

Yin-Chin and Bobby are set free

that was in the dark. The only exciting thing I remember on the road to Delhi was when we were suddenly jolted awake from our sleep by a big thud. The driver had hit a deer that had jumped in front of the car. The deer was stunned for a moment, then ran off into the woods. We were all relieved to see that it was okay. The car had only minor damage.

We arrived at the Taylors' home in the evening. Mrs. Taylor showed us where we would sleep. Bobby and I were each given our own bedroom and bathroom. We couldn't believe it when we saw how clean and tidy everything was. She told us to take a bath and join them for dinner. It was the most luxurious bath I had ever had: hot and cold running water, soft, clean, fluffy towels, soap and shampoo. It had been more than two and a half months since we had a hot bath. I could have stayed soaking in that warm water forever. Finally, we joined our hosts for dinner, chatted for a while, and then we were sent straight off to our different bedrooms. We had an early morning plane to catch. I was totally exhausted, feeling bad about leaving Papa and Popo behind, but at the same time excited to think how wonderful it would be to see our mother again. It didn't take long to fall asleep in the warm comfortable bed. The next day, awakened after a most wonderful sleep, we were given a hearty American breakfast. Mr. and Mrs. Taylor drove us to Delhi airport. We were grateful that they came to get us and couldn't thank them enough for what they did. We said our goodbyes and boarded Royal Nepal Airlines and were on our way to be reunited with our mother.

27

Plane to Kathmandu

Shortly before our release, the Commandant had started giving permission to the internees to request care packages from family members who had not been interned. Papa decided to write to my uncle in Calcutta and ask him to send us some things. He asked us what we needed. I remember requesting shoes for all of us since ours were completely tattered. We had only one pair, the shoes we were wearing at the time of our arrest. One or two weeks before we left camp we received a care package. In the package, among some other items, were three pairs of the ugliest brown canvas shoes I ever saw. Uncle sent each of us, except Popo, of course, a pair of shoes—all about two sizes too big. Under ordinary circumstances, I wouldn't have been caught dead wearing them, but we had no choice!

We had saved our best and cleanest clothes to wear on the day we would be set free. When our day came, Bobby and I put them on. They were the strangest outfits. He had on pants that were six inches too short and a shirt with missing buttons and sleeves that looked as if they had shrunk in the wash. Luckily, he still fitted into his wool coat, but it looked out of place in the desert. I had on a light blue woolen plaid skirt and matching vest, with a white blouse which had also shrunk. We both had on our brand new oversized brown canvas shoes!

Wearing this strange apparel, we arrived at Kathmandu airport in a DC-3, both feeling queasy from airsickness and from the excitement of seeing our mother again. We disembarked and saw her standing at the end of the airfield in front of the terminal building. We ran towards her and didn't stop until we were both in her arms.

It took many days to believe that we were actually free. I had so much to tell my mother but didn't know how to begin. Luckily, she did not push me to hear all the stories at once. The first thing she asked was why we hadn't come to Kathmandu when she had made it possible for us to do so. It had not been easy to make the arrangements, after all. She told us that she had fainted at the terminal when she learned we were not on the plane. Bobby looked at me with wide eyes, as if to say, "You were right in assuming this would happen." We were both apologetic and explained why we felt we could not come and expressed our hope that she would understand.

After the initial excitement of the reunion, we began to settle into our new surroundings. It was wonderful to see Borjee and Ayah again and they were both thrilled to see that we were all right. Ayah was particularly happy to see Bobby and told him how much she had missed him. They asked after Papa and Popo and hoped they would join us soon. It was good to see their old familiar faces. I enjoyed wandering around the hotel grounds and looking at all the greenery. It was towards the end of February and the camellias and other flowers were in bloom. It was a contrast to the stark environment of the internment camp.

The Imperial Hotel was what Mummy called her hotel. It was a two-storied old palace, badly rundown. She leased it and converted it into a twenty-five-room hotel with a full bar and a Chinese restaurant. She operated her hairdressing shop, Tika Beauty Salon, at one end of the second floor. It consisted of two large rooms. She converted one room into a salon and turned the second into her own living quarters. When we first arrived, Bobby and I shared her bed and waited for the room across the hall from her salon to become available, then moved into it. We finally felt at home and safe.

For those three weeks after we were reunited with our mother, I spent most of my time sitting or lying on the grass, just looking at everything. Bobby was busy scampering around. It felt as if we had gone to heaven. My mother decided that it was time we attended school again. She enrolled Bobby in a Catholic boys' school as a day student. She enrolled me in another boarding school called St. Mary's. I pleaded with her not to put me in boarding school again. I wanted to be home with her. She told me that she wanted me home too but was doing it for my own good. I complained every time my mother came to visit me at school and told her I might as well be back in the internment camp. I spent three unhappy months there.

Summer finally arrived and I was ecstatic to go home. Mummy took us on picnics and outings, trying to make up for lost time. We made many new friends, but as the summer drew to a close I began to dread the thought of returning to school. A week or ten days before the start of the school year, my mother surprised us by taking us to visit the American International School. She had decided to enroll us there, and told me that I would no longer be a boarder. Then she broke some startling news which she had been avoiding telling us from the time we first arrived. She said that she and our father had been having difficulties in their marriage over the past few years. There had been disagreements and other problems, including a couple of affairs he had had before she left India; she felt she no longer could live with him. We were shocked as she told us that she had filed for divorce. The papers were sent to him at camp to sign and she had recently received them back. Then, she said that she had been dating an American who was part of the U.S. diplomatic mission in Nepal for over a year: they were planning to marry. She felt that if we were to live in America, we should both become accustomed to American culture and their way of living.

It took some time for this news to sink in. I began to accept the inevitability of a new and changed life. Subsequently, we met my mother's future husband, whom we got to know well and liked; we felt that he would bring her happiness and security. She taught us how decent, open-minded, and generous the American people were and she was sure that we would love the new school. I was excited about attending the American school, but the first two weeks of school gave me a big shock. I had anticipated that the kids would be welcoming and friendly. Instead, they were quite the opposite. Since I was shy and still adjusting to all the changes, I didn't engage in conversation naturally. Many kids assumed I was stupid and didn't speak English. I never knew whether it was because I was Chinese or whether I was just "the new kid on the block". They made fun when I spoke. Perhaps I had more of an English accent than an American one. After several weeks in school, I became accustomed to the new ways and I was gradually accepted, but the experience eroded some of my initial naiveté. And while I was still excited about the prospect of moving to a new country, I was sad knowing that Papa would not be part of our new life.

Nine months later, we started our journey to America. Looking back, our departure was quite dramatic. On that day, there was a large crowd at Kathmandu airport to see us off. They included many diplomats, government officials, and a number of old customers and friends of my mother. All were in a jubilant mood and had come out to send us off in grand style with caviar and champagne. Everything was going well until we were called to board the plane. When we got up to the ticket counter, the immigration officer asked to see our entry documents. Alas, Bobby and I had none.

When we came into Nepal from Delhi the previous year on a routine Royal Nepal Airlines flight, the rules and regulations at the airport at that time were somewhat lax. The fact that all the pilots and airport officials knew my mother and were excited to see her reunited with her children, meant that no one had bothered to check for the normal entry documentation. Had they done so, they would have discovered that they were non-existent. Now that we were leaving, and airport procedures had become more formal, the lack of official entry papers was a big problem. Immigration would not allow us to leave without it.

A number of the people who had come to see us off sprang into action. A few got into a jeep and went back into town to the Foreign Office to meet with the Chief of

Protocol. Meanwhile, word of our plight had reached the control tower. Minutes later, an announcement came over the loud speaker, "The Control Tower has informed us that they are experiencing extreme and unsettled weather on the flight path. It is necessary to delay the departure of the flight to Calcutta. We ask passengers to return to the departure lounge and await further instructions. We apologize for the inconvenience." All the passengers disembarked and filed into the departure waiting area. They looked up at the perfectly blue sky and must have puzzled over the announcement.

The contingent that went to the Foreign Office returned two hours later with all the necessary documentation for departure and we were finally allowed to leave. This coincided with a remarkable improvement in the weather conditions and the plane finally took off.

We had an overnight layover in Calcutta. My father had been released from camp to Calcutta in April of 1964, just three months prior, so Mummy informed him that we were coming and arranged for us to meet. It had been a year since we left him at the camp and we were looking forward to seeing him before we left India. Bobby and I were thrilled to see him when he came to our hotel. He was so thin. He tried to keep up his sense of humour but looked sad.

It was both a bitter and sweet occasion. He had not seen my mother in three years and so many things had transpired. It was an amicable, but awkward, encounter. She introduced him to her new husband and the two men went off together to get acquainted. When they returned, Papa told us he would be having dinner with my mother and the two of us. Our stepfather had the sensitivity to let us spend our last time together without him. Papa also said he would spend the night with Bobby and me, which delighted us, of course. That night in our room, he tried to convince us that he was happy we were getting a chance for a new life. He found our stepfather to be a kind and decent man who promised that he would take care of us as if we were his own children. Papa reassured us that he would be okay and not to worry about him.

The following morning we boarded the airport bus in front of the hotel and I took a window seat. As the bus pulled away, I looked at my father standing at the curb looking forlorn. With a heavy heart and tears streaming down my face, I waved goodbye. As he waved back, I wondered what was going to become of him.

Epilogue

My brother and I were the first prisoners to be released from the Deoli camp. The remaining internees were released intermittently until the camp closed in 1967, five years after they had first been interned. The Indian government prohibited internees from returning to their homes where they had been living before they were arrested and exiled. This meant that they lost all their businesses and property. Those lucky enough to have homes or relatives in other parts of India relocated in an attempt to start life over.

In the interim, China found out that the Indian government had interned ethnic Chinese. In a move designed to enhance its standing and further shame the Indian government, China decided to open her arms and "welcome back" her people. Many internees accepted the offer and returned—or went for the first time—to China; they deeply resented how the Indian government had treated them. Others, who had been rendered virtually homeless, felt they had little choice other than to return to China. They hoped they would be well received.

Another group of internees—initially afraid to go to China because of their past anti-Communist sentiments and allegiance to the Nationalist government—felt their chances of survival might still prove better in China than in India. They returned, however, with some apprehension.

Finally, there were those, like my father, who refused to accept China's invitation because of their political affiliations and felt that their philosophical differences were irreconcilable. They remained in India until life became intolerable.

When I asked my mother why we were the first ones to be freed, she told us that it was due to the efforts of many friends—one in particular, someone my parents had gotten to know in Darjeeling. He was an international correspondent who had been living and working on the subcontinent for many years; he was there during the time of China's invasion of Tibet. Because of his direct involvement with the issues of Tibet, and his continued writings about India's initial lack of support of Tibet and the border regions of India, he became a thorn in Prime Minister Nehru's side. Eventually, he was declared persona non grata. When my mother contacted him and told him what had happened to her family, this gentleman was outraged and promised to do whatever he could to help. He wrote to Prime Minister Nehru and expressed his deep concern about the treatment of the Chinese, specifically raising the issue of our family. He indicated that he felt so strongly about this that he was prepared to bring public attention to it. Nehru, who had in the past experienced the power of this reporter's pen, decided to free just the two of us.

* * *

After my brother and I were freed, my grandmother stayed on in the camp for another six months. Finally, she was released due to poor health. Since she could not return to Darjeeling, she went to live with her son and grandson in Calcutta.

The Foreigners Act and Order issued by the government in November of 1962 gave licence to the native Indian population to harass the ethnic Chinese in many different ways. My cousin told me later that he felt his life was in danger each time he went to and from school. Chinese children were forced to travel to school in a convoy for their own protection and a Chinese individual caught alone in the street was often beaten; some even lost their lives. Life had become too difficult, unpleasant and dangerous for the Chinese in India, so my uncle, cousin, and Popo decided to leave. They emigrated to Taiwan in 1963. We never saw Popo again. She died in 1972.

My father was interned in Deoli for fifteen months; since he had also spent time in the Darjeeling jail, he had been incarcerated for a total of sixteen months. Never formally accused or indicted, he lost all his property and business in Darjeeling and was forbidden to ever return. He had no choice but to move back to Calcutta. Luckily, he had his flat to return to after his release. Many people did not have this choice. My father continued to live in Calcutta for about three years, struggling to make a living in what had become a hostile environment for a Chinese national. A friend found him a job as a journalist for a Chinese newspaper but his heart was not in it after the break up of his family. He felt alone and isolated, and finally decided to leave India. He asked my older sister, who had remained in the U.S. after college, to sponsor his moving there. When it came time to emigrate, he had no money or possessions. He signed his ninety-nine-year lease of our flat (which he had kept since the days of his import-export business) over to the owner of the dry-cleaning shop on the bottom floor of our building, and purchased a one-way plane ticket to America.

When my sister went to meet him in Baltimore in 1967, my father arrived with just the clothes on his back. He eventually moved to the Chicago area and settled there, remarrying and starting a new life. He became an American citizen, worked hard with his new family, and lived out his life in peace and comfort.

I visited my father, and took my children to meet him, from time to time over the years but I was never able to have the same connection we once had. Ironically, it was in Deoli internment camp that we were the closest—a fleeting moment. My father died in 2003.

My mother lived happily in her new life in the United States for six years. Sadly, she passed away in 1970 from leukaemia and was not present to see me graduate from university in 1971. I later married an American Foreign Service Officer and we lived in many parts of the world before settling down in the San Francisco Bay Area. We have two grown children who live and work in California. My brother also married and has two grown children. My older sister continues to live in Virginia with her children and grandchildren.

Fortunately, with the passage of time and maturity, I have overcome the anger that had been bottled up in me for years. I feel the Indian culture still ingrained in me, and Indian food is still very much a part of our diet. When I enter an

Indian grocery store and smell the spices, I unconsciously start waggling my head and speaking English with an Indian cadence.

My feeling of anger, however, has been replaced with a feeling of sadness over the unjust way the Chinese in India were treated. I also remain disturbed that this shameful chapter in India's history has been successfully suppressed for fifty years. It is an ironic and sad commentary that while the India–China Border War lasted just about a month, the internment camp remained open for five and a half years.

I hope this memoir encourages other internees to tell their stories, and that one day soon, the Government of India will see fit to make an official apology to the Chinese Indian community for the decades of shame, suffering, and loss they were forced to undergo.

Appendix
Historical Background

Relations between India and China (mid-1800s–1962)

Before 1962, India's government and native population did not generally resent the Chinese in their country. The numbers of Chinese nationals were small and they carried little political weight. In addition, the Chinese accepted jobs that the Indians did not want; therefore, the Chinese did not present a threat.

After India gained its independence from Britain in 1947, and the Communists established a new regime in China in 1949, these emerging nations shared a common bond and envisioned a new Asia built in part on an alliance between their two countries. The decade of the 1950s was commonly referred to as the "Nehru–Chou En Lai Honeymoon"; a popular expression of the day was "Hindi Chini Bhai Bhai", meaning "Indians and Chinese are brothers". The Indian government was among the first to recognize the People's

Republic of China as the new legitimate government, and encouraged Chinese living in India to register for citizenship with the P.R.C.

The honeymoon period was short-lived, however, and soon deteriorated with the increasing tension between the two countries over border territory. This disagreement came to the forefront in the late 1950s and early '60s, culminating in a border war in 1962. Though the war lasted only a month, the residual effects on the relations between the two countries have lasted decades and still ferment.

The Chinese living in India suffered greatly as a result of this conflict. The steady increase of Chinese emigration into India came to a halt because of the deteriorating relationship between the two governments, and the Chinese, whose

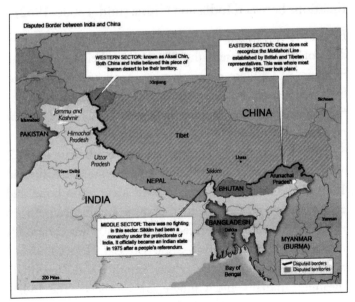

The India-China Border

families may have lived in India for several generations, began to leave India to seek stability and a home elsewhere.

Border between India and China

The total length of the border between India and China is about 2,500 miles. It was never defined or officially drawn up until the late 1800s when the British did so. They saw Russia and China as emerging competing powers and were eager to create buffer zones to protect their own encroachment into India. The border areas fall into three sections: Western, Central, and Eastern.

The Western sector spans about 1,000 miles from Afghanistan to Nepal. The disputed area in this section totals about 15,000 square miles and includes part of the Ladakh Desert region known as the Aksai Chin ("white stone desert"). The Aksai Chin is more than a hundred miles across and roughly 17,000 feet in elevation. Over the centuries the Chinese government had always considered these border territories between India and China as belonging to Tibet, and ultimately, under its domain. The Aksai Chin was declared British (Indian) territory by W.H. Johnson, an officer of the Survey of India, and re-established in 1897 by Major General Sir John Ardagh, Director of Military Intelligence of the British General Staff. China, however, never recognized what became known as the Johnson/Ardagh Line.

The Middle sector included three Himalayan Kingdoms: Nepal, Bhutan and Sikkim. At the time the Johnson-Ardagh Line was drawn, each of these countries had independent relationships with the two larger countries that surround them. Though there are nearly 400 miles of disputed border in this sector, no actual fighting took place there during the 1962 conflict.

The Eastern sector of these border regions—where most of the fighting of the 1962 war took place—spans about 700 miles along the Himalayan crest between Bhutan and Burma. The Indians called this area of approximately 32,000–35,000 square miles, the North East Frontier Agency (NEFA). The Chinese and Tibetans have always recognized this area as part of Tibet. Since the late 1800s British colonialists have wanted this region to serve as another buffer zone between India and China.

In 1913 the British colonial government in India called together the Simla Conference. They invited representatives from China and Tibet. The chief British delegate, Arthur Henry McMahon presented the McMahon Line which

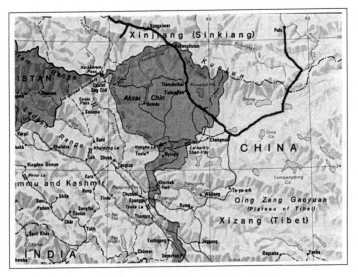

Aksai Chin and the Western border conflict

pushed British territory from the foothills of Assam all the way to the Himalayan Crest.

The British set the timing of the conference to coincide with the collapse of the Ching dynasty and the founding of the Nationalist government. Consequently, no official representatives were sent from China, and although a local Chinese delegate did attend and initial the proposal, there was no formal signature or recognition from the new government in China. Representatives from Tibet, who did attend, came to the conference hoping that the British would help them gain independence from China. With signatures of both Tibetan and Indian officials, but none from China, the McMahon Line was made official, but it has never been recognized by China as legitimate.

Several reasons forced the claims and arguments of the border to the forefront by the late 1950s. First, the Chinese had begun to build a road from Sinkiang to Tibet. It spanned approximately 100 miles through Aksai Chin and simplified

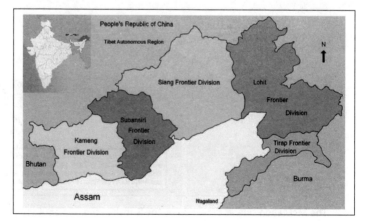

NEFA (Northeast Frontier Agency) and the Eastern border conflict.

travel between these two regions. Local residents, however, were suspicious about the real motivation for the Chinese road-building operation, suspecting that it had more to do with moving Chinese families into regions of Tibet in order to expedite colonization than it was created for ease of travel and trade.

India learned about the highway in 1958. A government patrol sent to investigate in Aksai Chin went missing and India sent a note to Beijing on October 18, 1958, inquiring about it, claiming that the patrol had been on Indian Territory. China responded three weeks later on November 8 that the patrol was deported because it was found on Chinese territory. This event brought the disagreements over the Aksai Chin to the forefront.

When the P.R.C. took control in 1950, Tibet declared its independence and China responded by invading Tibet. To India, this further aggravation in Sino–Indian relations was seen as a threat towards its government. The Tibetan rebellion

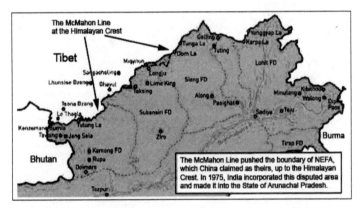

The McMahon Line as drawn up by the British in the mid-1800s pushed the border up to the Himalayan crest

spread; China launched a full-scale assault on Tibet in 1959 and squelched the rebellion, taking full control of the region. Thousands of Tibetans were killed and the Dalai Lama was encouraged by his people to flee. India immediately offered the Dalai Lama and thousands of other Tibetan refugees political asylum. China saw this gesture as a direct attack on its government. These combined factors abruptly ended the decade-long honeymoon period between the two countries.

When China took Tibet, India became increasingly uneasy and sent troops to the disputed borders to protect its own territorial claims. China did the same. Arguments and attempted negotiations over the border continued. At one point, China offered to comply with India's claim to the NEFA area in return for total control of the disputed area in the Aksai Chin, which would enable them to maintain control of their newly built highway.

India was unwilling to negotiate since it felt that the McMahon Line already delineated the territory. Between 1960–62 there was a steady build-up of troop patrols on both sides in Aksai Chin and NEFA. A number of small skirmishes took place where each side lost lives, but no compromise could be reached. On October 20, 1962 China and India went to war.

A month later, after the loss of many lives on both sides, China declared a unilateral ceasefire and the war ended. China was momentarily satisfied that it had reached the lines of the border they had claimed. They moved back about twenty kilometers from the McMahon Line and established a border checkpoint. It seemed a reasonable compromise at the time. One of the fallouts that resulted from the border war was anti-Chinese legislation in India, including the Foreigners Law Act passed in November 26, 1962, and Foreigners Order issued January 14, 1963.

India defined "foreigner" as "any person who—or whose parents, or grandparents, had been—at any time a citizen or subject of any country at war with, or committing external aggression against India." The Act restricted the freedom of movement of people of Chinese descent and required them to carry a permit whenever they left their registered address for more than twenty-four hours. It also restricted Chinese from leaving India except under the rules of the Act. Once given permission, Chinese ethnics were further restricted from leaving India by air or sea, except from Calcutta, Madras, Bombay, and New Delhi. The Chinese were also required to specify the details of any travel plans.

The Foreigners Order required ethnic Chinese to carry a permit at all times to live in, or even enter, particular restricted areas near the border in the State of Assam and some districts of West Bengal like Darjeeling and Kalimpong, Uttar Pradesh, and Punjab. Many Chinese who were residents of these restricted areas were forced from their homes.

For a number of years after the border war and after the Foreigners Order was issued, life became intolerable for ethnic Chinese living in India. Those who were able to leave, emigrated to other parts of the world, mostly to Canada, the United States, and Australia. Today, there are only a few hundred ethnic Chinese who remained in India. They were finally naturalized as citizens in 1998.

References

Books and Other Publications

Cohen, Jerome Alan and Shao-Chuan Leng. 1972. *The Sino-Indian Dispute Over the Internment and Detention of Chinese Nationals.* Cambridge: Harvard University Press.

Marsh, Nicole. 1998. 'Chinese Internment in India, 1962–1967: Through the Oral'. Unpublished Master's thesis, University of California, Santa Cruz.

Maxwell, Neville. 1970. *India's China War.* New York: Pantheon Books.

Oxfeld, Ellen. 1993. *Blood, Seat, and Mahjong: Family and Enterprise in an Overseas Chinese Community.* New York: Cornell University Press.

Maps

Acknowledgements

The process of writing my memoir took much longer than I had ever anticipated. After plugging away at it for three years, I was becoming weary of editing my own work and not completely happy with the stage I was in. I was introduced to Jannie Dresser who was just the sort of editor I was looking for. Jannie has continually asked questions about events that were unclear and encouraged me to "flesh out the story." By the completion of the manuscript, I have become totally familiar with the term and am finally satisfied with the outcome. I am most grateful to her.

I would also especially like to thank my daughter Nicole, who not only gave me invaluable advice and guidance during the time I was writing but also accompanied me, along with my son Rex, on our 2001 trip to Calcutta and Darjeeling. They gave me the moral and emotional support I needed to remember and revisit these traumatic events of my life.

I also wish to express my appreciation to my husband, Noel, for being completely supportive throughout the entire process and putting up with the roller-coaster ride of emotions that were evoked when delving into the past. And, I am thankful to my brother, Bobby, for coming up with the sketches. I had given him a copy of one of my first drafts to read. He read it through the night and when he was done, got paper and pencil and started making sketches of the camp. His sketches mirrored what I had in my mind. I was impressed. He was only eight when we were interned.

Finally, I wish to acknowledge the advice and encouragement I have received from my friends and family who read my first drafts.